DATE DUE

248.2
EPS
    Epstein, Kathie.
       The quiet riot

First Baptist Church Library
Elk City, Oklahoma

DEMCO

The
Quiet Riot

248.2
Eps

The Quiet Riot

Kathie Epstein

Fleming H. Revell Company
Old Tappan, New Jersey

Unless otherwise identified, Scripture quotations are from The Living Bible, Copyright © 1971 by Tyndale House Publishers, Wheaton, Illinois 60187. All rights reserved.

Scripture quotations identified KJV are from the King James Version of the Bible.

Scripture quotations identified PHILLIPS are from THE NEW TESTAMENT IN MODERN ENGLISH (Revised Edition), translated by J.B. Phillips. © J.B. Phillips 1958, 1960, 1972. Used by permission of Macmillan Publishing Co., Inc.

Library of Congress Cataloging in Publication Data

Epstein, Kathie.
    The quiet riot.

    1. Epstein, Kathie. I. Title.
BR1725.E66A36   248'.2'0924 [B]   76-2719
ISBN 0-8007-0789-3

Copyright © 1976 Fleming H. Revell Company
All rights reserved
Printed in the United States of America

TO my parents
who prove every day that the essence of love
is the unconditional giving of self
and
TO Carlton
who proves every day that the essence
of friendship is exactly the same

Contents

Foreword

Though at twenty-two Kathie Epstein may be one of America's youngest authors, she's used to seeing her name in print. I know—because it appears in my own four latest books!

For the past several years Kathie has twinkled in and out of our household—and our hearts and lives—like our own small shooting star. Eyes shining, long dark hair flying, she zooms in and energizes everyone around—Bob, me, the kids, people on the phone, even the cat. She is as healthy and delicious as fresh-squeezed vitamin C—and coming from the Florida orange juice gal, that's really a compliment!

Bob and I discovered Kathie at America's Junior Miss Pageant in Mobile, Alabama. As I autographed copies of *Mine Eyes Have Seen the Glory,* my first book, for the girls, certainly I didn't dream one of them—the winsome miss representing Maryland—would appear in our future books: *Amazing Grace, Bless This House, Fishers of Men, Light My Candle.*

As we came to know Kathie during the exciting days preceding the pageant, Bob soon learned the most important thing about her: Kathie Epstein is a radiant, believing Christian!

And because he relates well to youngsters, he soon knew a lot more about this one: about her "fantastic" parents, whom Kathie described as "sold out to the Lord"; big brother David and little sister Michie; and the extraordinary respect, closeness, and tenderness this family so naturally shares.

Of course Bob knew Kathie could sing—in fact, some call her another Anita Bryant!—and he became interested in her obvious talent. But then he learned something so odd, so singular, it could only be called a tremendous "God-incidence"; Kathie and her mother were to attend the same Conference on Biblical Prophecy which we planned to attend—in Jerusalem, Israel. "God found us a baby-sitter," Bob told me, amazed.

Baby-sitter, yes—at first. Later, however, Kathie joined us at Villa Verde as secretary, baby-sitter, errand girl, surrogate daughter. She helped teach the twins to swim; smashed a fender on our car; read stories to Bobby and Gloria; wrote me a poem; designed and stitched a beautiful wall-hanging for our kitchen; and with Michie, worked like a trooper during the hectic weeks of our Anita Bryant Summer Camp for Girls.

What does Kathie (Kaffy Kake, the kids call her) mean to our home? Well, the Lord sent her to us to love, first of all. For me, she represented a beautiful model of the sort of decent, fine teenager Christian parents hope to produce.

For Bob, the Lord used Kathie in a special way when she became his first show-business protégée. He helped her obtain the professional bookings that began her Christian show-business career—and from that beginning, the Lord and Bob and Kathie put together Bob's now thriving Christian talent agency, Fishers of Men Opportunities, Inc.

The Quiet Riot will tell you a lot more about this very real girl, who really will go places for the Lord. Singer, writer, artist, witness for Jesus, devoted daughter, sister, and friend—Kathie epitomizes the sort of joyous, talented, turned-on person we all admire.

Obviously, Bob and I love Kathie. Our kids love Kathie. And so do Kathie's peers—the young people to whom she witnesses and with whom she lives and works and plays.

But most important of all, Jesus loves Kathie Epstein—and her life proves it as she continues to perform and speak and shine for Him.

ANITA BRYANT

Preface

Change is simultaneously the most exciting and frightening experience. Each time we face a new encounter with change we agonize over the fear of it, and yet we are mysteriously attracted to its promise of greater reward. I grew up in a time in history when *change* was almost considered synonymous with *revolution.* It was a tense period of sharp criticism and cutting reevaluation of traditional morality and life-style. As a young person I was literally forced through peer pressure to decide which moral road I would travel and which end of the political spectrum I would embrace. Strangely enough, neither school of philosophy seemed attractive to me. I felt that both extremes led to emotional and psychological bondage—the exact opposite of their promised results!

Then I found Jesus and He changed everything. Jesus has a terrific way of putting everything into its proper perspective. I no longer needed a social cause for which to fight or a political flag to wave.

This book was written primarily as a testimony to the joy I have found in having a personal and vital relationship with the living Christ. It is also written as an encouragement to young people who have grown up in the church, and as a result of this advantage, are expected to have instant solutions to life's problems. Today's youth wants answers. They are no longer satisfied with their parents' evaluations; they want to find out for themselves. I know.

I know because I, too, am young, grew up in the church, and have had to face the incredible pressure to join the "revolution generation." Every young person alive experiences one sort of revolution or another as they pass through the delicate transition into adulthood. They are torn between their traditional values and the tempting allure of the "new morality." They question the significance of a two-thousand-year-old religion to their young lives in such a modern, mechanized society. I think they have cause to wonder, for religion is not what's happening at all. But Jesus is!

I, too, have experienced change in many directions during my twenty-two years. Most of it has been exciting, much of it has been frustrating and disappointing, but *all* of it has been frightening! I thank the Good Lord that I have emerged from it a wiser human being, a more confident woman, and a more sincere and joyful Christian.

My life has been more riotous than revolutionary—a "quiet riot." I have been faced with the same temptations, disillusionments, and searching questions as every other young person alive today. And I know that it is impossible to bear it alone. The good news is that we as young people and as children of God have a wonderful friend with whom we can bear it together.

But remember this—the wrong desires that come into your life aren't anything new and different. Many others have faced exactly the same problems before you. And no temptation is irresistible. You can trust God to keep the temptation from becoming so strong that you can't stand up against it, for he has promised this and will do what he says. He will show you how to escape temptation's power so that you can bear up patiently against it.

1 Corinthians 10:13

And that's a promise!

The
Quiet Riot

1

First Love

*Let everyone bless God and sing his praises, for he holds
our lives in his hands. And he holds our feet to the path.
You have purified us with fire, O Lord, like silver in a
crucible.*

Psalms 66:8–10

I was fifteen. He was nineteen and all the things first
loves are made of: tall and slender and tanned so deep no
winter's pale approached him. Blonde curls formed a halo
around a face already too angelic to need one, and his eyes
were a deeper blue than the sea he loved so much. Yancy
and the sea—they were inseparable—they were one. I
was just a foreigner in their world and I resented their
devotion to each other.

At a time when I was newly awakened to the wonder
of my womanhood, it seemed unfair that my greatest
competition, Mother Ocean, should claim Yancy's prime
affection. How I envied her beauty, her magic, her mystery. With every wave his surfboard caught he seemed to
fall in love with her all over again, possessed more surely
than before.

I really think we could have made it, Yancy and I. I understood him, and Yancy needed lots of understanding. As completely as the sea had enslaved him, I, too, became a slave to my love for Yancy. Obsession of any sort can be a disastrous thing and, too young and innocent to foresee the consequences, I plunged more deeply month by month into the ecstasy of my love. I idolized him, I idealized him. And frankly, I just about killed him with kindness. I think the shock of so much affection completely unnerved him.

I can only blame it on my childhood. I was born into one of those rare homes of infinite love and attention, complete with wonderful parents who even planned me! Love was a way of life, and affection was as much a certainty as three meals a day. My father was in the Navy at the time I was born, stationed near Paris, France. The world I awakened to was one filled with the warmth of the sunshine that poured through the windows of our converted-barn house on the outskirts of the city of love, itself. My folks were the type who made friends easily. They didn't move into a foreign country and then attempt to Americanize the life-style; they found a charm about the local people and embraced the French way of life as their own. Every morning Mom would find fresh vegetables and flowers on our doorstep. Our predecessor had been greeted each day with garbage strewn across the lawn—a French acknowledgment of his "superiority." When we finally moved to the United States my mother even gave her washing machine to our neighbor!

What kind of chance did I have? I had an older brother,

David, who was three when I was born. It didn't matter
to him in the least that I wasn't a boy—he made me
an all-American in every sport by the time I was two anyway! "Day-Day," as I called him then out of necessity and
now call him out of choice, became my great protec-
tor and counselor. Together we conquered the neighborhood.

That's enough right there to plead my case, but the
birth of my younger sister clinched it when I was twenty
months old. Michie came into the world "behind" first
and I have been trying to straighten her out ever since!
We share a great friendship—rare among sisters—and
have learned a great deal from our life together. Add to
all this a dog named Zorro with the sweetest disposition
possible, and that completes the loving atmosphere of my
childhood. I rest my case!

Now you can understand that it was only natural for me
to smother Yancy with all the love I'd been showered with
for fifteen years. Only he wasn't conditioned for it as I had
been! I want you to understand that it wasn't a case of his
not loving me, he did. He loved me as much as he could
under the circumstances.

Yancy was on his way to really making it big in a field
where few make it at all—professional surfing. There is an
art to this sport; it's a graceful flight of gymnastic perfection that unites man and nature in an experience too
beautiful to describe. At least Yancy never could describe
it. But his eyes always betrayed what his lips could not,
and somehow I grew to empathize with his passion for the
water. Even during the long months of waiting to hear
from him, I still understood.

I felt imprisoned in the winter routine of classes and schedules. Pensacola, Florida seemed an eternity removed from my chilly Maryland suburb. But Yancy always seemed right there. I'd never been one to date a lot —I ran home crying the first time a seventh-grader kissed me—and high school only served to set me more in my ways. I was a one-man woman and Yancy was the one man. That is, he *was* until he wrote me that he had found another woman!

Kathie—

What I have to tell you is very hard, but maybe you were expecting it . . . please try to understand, but with you a thousand miles away the odds were against us from the beginning and I was not strong enough. Please forgive me for what I have done, but I will have to suffer in the long run.

YANCY

Well, I don't give up easily. After treating my family to torrents of tears and melancholy moods, I decided I would wait it out until Yancy finally came to his senses and realized he couldn't live without me. He did.

Spring arrived and the warm weather somehow found us together again. I can't even begin to recall the times we continued in the cycle that the young are so famous for! We couldn't live with each other or without each other. I was fast becoming a nervous wreck with a craving for sweets and a passion for long hours in silent communication with my stereo.

I am convinced that the most pathetic thing about my love affair with Yancy is that I wasted so much precious time. I allowed another human being to become so important to me that I neglected to nurture priceless relationships with my family and friends. I could think of nothing else but the time when we would finally be together—this time for good. I kept thinking that if we'd only have more time together than the summer offered we would find a way to make it work. Autumn soon became my fiercest foe.

Wow, I really blew those years. They were supposed to be the greatest years of my life, and I let them slip by me as if I had them to live over again. None of us do, you know.

I've learned now that each day is a gift too valuable to waste in self-pity and regret. I have a plaque in my apartment that advises: DON'T FILL YOUR LIFE WITH YEARS: FILL YOUR YEARS WITH LIFE! If only we could realize early in life how swiftly our youth passes and how quickly our beauty fades, then we would know to fatten our days with the things that last: the joy of awakening to the splendors of this earth; good times spent with good friends in good fellowship; and bringing a ray of happiness into the lives of those who have never seen the sunshine. I guess it's easy to talk about. Very few of us actually put it into practice.

And that brings me back to Yancy. I had already made my family miserable for months, but now I was beginning to feel real guilt for the grief I was causing. Sure, I was a

Christian—or at least I thought I was. I had accepted Jesus Christ as my Saviour when I was eleven. Going forward after a showing of the Billy Graham film "The Restless Ones," I had asked Him into my heart. So, He was my Saviour already, but a long way from being Lord of my life! I guess I just wanted Jesus to fit real neatly into the life I had already chosen for myself—no discomfort, no rearranging of my character, no sacrifice of self. Real comfortable. You know, like instant soup—instant Saviour! How sterile! I don't think there is anything more useless than a stagnant religion. The churches are full of it and it's turning off young people by the droves. I don't blame them for rejecting it! If something doesn't meet your needs, who needs it?

So I reached the point where I could hardly face myself in the mirror any longer. What a hypocrite I'd become! I was a self-righteous Penelope Purity who was actually more deceitful than the young people out on the streets who were shouting *love, peace, brotherhood* with one breath and throwing bombs with the next. I was more hypocritical because I pretended to believe in something that my life did not reflect. I read 1 Corinthians 13 and realized that I did not have that kind of love in my life— that kind of love didn't torture those who loved me with worry and fear. That kind of love didn't brood for hours in gloomy despair, and that kind of love didn't puff itself up with pride over being "good." My kind of love was jealous, self-centered, and destructive. So it wasn't even love at all, just an ugly lie. It was idolatry; and there's nothing God despises more than idolatry, whatever form it takes.

Wow! It was as if I'd been knocked over the head by an archangel himself! I rededicated my life to Jesus and asked Him to reign supreme in every detail of my life: to guide my steps, establish my relationships, and dwell within all my decisions. Jesus wanted to live in my heart *and* in my mind. The heart responded easily to His message of love. But my mind was stubborn—it resisted any interference, especially from an Unseen Force. I don't know about you, but God hasn't appeared to me physically yet!

The climax came when I finally surrendered Yancy to the Lord, body and soul. It really was a battle, but when I raised that little flag signaling my defeat, it turned into a great victory for me and God.

I hardly dreamed that would be the beginning of more problems! No sooner had I recommited my life to Jesus than my whole world began to crumble around me. It was the fall of my senior year in high school, and one by one the things most precious to me fell apart. My best friend (since third grade) suddenly went the hippie route and I no longer fit into her life. Then followed a series of incidents that seem trivial now but, at the time, were incredibly important. To top it off, Yancy broke up with me for the fifth (Or was it the fiftieth?) time, and that was about all I could take.

"If this is Christianity—you can have it!" I stormed at my mother, sobs overcoming me. I guess I secretly blamed her for my troubles. She was always the one who told me I was miserable because Christ wasn't first in my life. Well, now He was first and I was more miserable than ever!

Her response was not quite as I expected. "You keep quiet and get down on your knees and you start praising Him for a change! I'm tired of your acting like a Christian only when it suits your mood. For once go beyond what *you* want and do what *He* says to do: *Thank Him!*"

I couldn't believe my ears. I thought Mom would shower me with sympathy, and here she was making matters worse! But she was in one of those immovable states, so I obediently got down on my knees and began to praise: "Thanks, God, for all the lousy things You've let happen to me. I really am grateful. It's so great to be miserable for Your sake." At this point I checked on Mom's reaction and it wasn't too favorable, so I altered my strategy and prayed: "Really, Lord, I'm sorry I can't see Your hand in all this. I need Your help and I can't make it without Your strength. I really do love You, Jesus. Please forgive me for not trusting You." All of a sudden I knew I was really sincere—I was actually thanking Him for my situation and actually meaning it! Relief flooded all through me.

"You see, Kath, God is like a Goldsmith who works over His precious pot of gold, melting it and stirring it and tending it. Nothing is more important to Him than His craft, and He knows the exact temperature to allow it to reach before it will burn from too much heat. When it's finally done—it's been through the fire, tested, and retested—the Goldsmith looks down into the pot and can see His reflection. That's when He knows His precious metal is ready to be molded into His purpose for it."

"It's a painful process," I said, feeling the flames around me even then.

"But, it's worth it." She smiled as she said, "Believe me —no—believe the Goldsmith!"

2

A Case for Virginity

*My darling bride is like a private garden, a spring that
no one else can have, a fountain of my own.*

Song of Solomon 4:12

All my life I had been warned of the evils of giving
myself sexually to a man prior to the marriage bed. I was
so naive that it hardly crossed my mind that the possibility
even existed! *Me—the girl who can't even enjoy kissing
games at parties?* The idea was incredulous. Until I fell in
love. Suddenly it seemed to me the most natural thing in
the world to make love with Yancy. Everything in me
longed to be given to him, regardless of right or wrong.
Who cared, anyway? Most of the "good" girls in school
had been at it for years, and nobody seemed to think any
less of them. *Why should I be any different?* At least I
could say with complete honesty that I was in love with
Yancy and hoped to marry him. *What's a ceremony matter when I'm already married in my heart?*

"You're a fool, Kathie." My mother was counseling
again, always there with an encouraging word. "A boy

who gets what he wants only gets tired of it and goes looking for fresh territory someplace else." We were sitting at our usual place, the kitchen table, having our usual cups of afternoon tea. I had just received a "Let's try again, Kath" letter from Yancy and I wasn't in the mood for a maternal sermon. I could tell Mom was far from excited about my plans to visit Yancy in Florida during Christmas vacation.

"Kathie, sex is a beautiful thing," she started, "but only within the sacred bonds of marriage. Don't sell yourself short, honey, the Lord has so much in store for you if you'll only wait on Him."

Wait! That is without a doubt the most distasteful word in my vocabulary. Hadn't I already *waited* a year and a half to finally visit Pensacola and meet Yancy's family? I felt like we'd been through more in that time than lots of couples experience in a lifetime. And so far we had managed to survive without a bit of sex. Looking back on it now, I can hardly believe it myself! We'd sure had enough opportunities, but something always seemed to interrupt us—just when things were beginning to get interesting. I was starting to wonder if I even turned him on at all. When I asked him about it he just smiled and said, "For sure, Kathryn." I was doomed to loving a guy who respected me! Have you ever felt like you'd like a little less respect and a lot more passion?

"Mom, I really love Yancy. I've been strong before and I'll be strong over Christmas, too." I took her hand to convince her. "Quit worrying and start *trusting!*" Boy, it was great to be on the preaching end for a change!

Through lots of prayer and pleading, I somehow managed to find myself in Pensacola on December 27, 1970. I was totally convinced that, away from the familiar atmosphere of home and family, Yancy and I would finally get it together. Absolutely nothing could have prepared me for the shock that greeted me there.

"Kathryn, I'm really glad you came. Your being here has helped me to see that I'm in love with Pam."

Pam? Who the heck was Pam? We were parked beside the bay in Yancy's Volkswagen. The rain was slashing against the windows, but all of a sudden there was more water in the car than out! Yancy took me in his arms to comfort me.

"Yancy, I can't believe that I'm losing you," I sobbed, burying my face in his chest.

"You can't lose anything you never had, Kathryn." His answer pierced clean through me, yet I knew he was right. You cannot own another human being, and I was guilty of trying to do just that. It was one of the hardest lessons I have ever had to learn.

"Okay Yance," I said, wiping my eyes in embarrassment. I threw back my waist-length hair to symbolize my acceptance. "I wish you happiness. That's all I ever wanted for you, anyway." How dramatic can you get? My family's nickname for me—Sarah Heartburn—seemed particularly appropriate that day. I was playing the part to the hilt.

Once I had recovered from the shock I reasoned that it was just another of Yancy's little flings, and he'd get over it as he always had before. Even his mother thought so, and mothers are never wrong. At least my mother never seems to be!

I remember getting up early one morning in Florida and making breakfast for Yancy and his little brother. I was busy with the oatmeal and they were killing time before the TV when suddenly I heard a familiar voice from the set. I looked up to see the current America's Junior Miss advertising the upcoming pageant. My heart went straight to my throat.

"Kathryn, have you ever entered one of those things?" Yancy asked, coming over to inspect my progress with the oatmeal.

"Well," I gulped, "as a matter of fact, I did—once. You all ready for breakfast?" I dropped the subject and pretended to be real busy, but Yancy noticed my uneasiness and faced me with the inevitable question.

"Yeah? When?"

I couldn't conceal it any longer. I had dreaded the moment when he would discover I had entered the pageant. And now the moment was here.

"I won the Bowie Junior Miss Pageant about two months ago and I go to the Maryland Pageant next month —your oatmeal's getting cold." I knew he was disappointed in me. Yancy felt that all beauty pageants were ego trips. I never understood how they were any different from his surf contests, except that he claimed those had nothing to do with physical beauty, just ability. I knew I would never be able to explain to him that the Junior Miss competition was based almost entirely on scholastic achievement, talent, and personality. As far as he was concerned, if it was called a pageant, it had to be an ego trip. His mind was closed.

"I'm going surfing."

I spent a week in Pensacola and grew to love Yancy's family. They were truly wonderful to me, and I could sense that they, too, hoped Yancy and I would work things out.

"Yancy's afraid of you, Kathie," his mom told me one day, not too long after our moment of truth in the Volkswagen. "He loves what you are—what you stand for—but he knows that he just can't live up to those standards himself." You can bet by now I was sick of sainthood! All I wanted was Yancy, and if being pure and noble was keeping us apart, then I was ready to dump it! I didn't have much time left to do it; I was scheduled to leave for Maryland in three days.

You can imagine the state of confusion I lived in those final days. I was literally ripped apart by fear and frustration, guilt and desire. My conscience taunted me with the possible consequences, but my heart ached to express all the passion of waiting so long to love and be loved. So my decision was made: I had already sinned in my mind, so why be hypocritical and keep my body from following in like fashion? Don't look up that kind of rationalization in your Bible—it isn't there unless it's in the "Book of Fools."

"Yance, can we go to Tyler's garage so I can see everybody?" Tyler's garage had fascinated me for months—it was *the* place and had more mystery surrounding it than an Agatha Christie novel. I was dying to finally see it and hoped that Yancy would suggest it. So when he didn't, I did! Somehow I talked him into it, and we arrived around ten o'clock that evening to be greeted by the unmistakable aroma of marijuana. Suddenly I was sure I preferred a quiet evening at home, but it was too late now.

"Hey, hi, Kathie." "Hello, Kathie." So many familiar faces filled the tiny garage apartment. It seemed strange to see my summer friends in such a foreign atmosphere. Of course, it wasn't foreign to them, this was their home nine months out of the year. Their three-month stay in the north every summer was just a vacation. Now our roles were switched; I was the foreigner invading *their* territory!

Soon we were settled into some soft cushions and I had my first chance to look around at the notorious place. Surfing posters, candles, rock music—not too mysterious. I'd seen a dozen just like it. But drugs had never been as abundant in my neighborhood as they seemed to be here. Yancy later told me that Pensacola was a distribution point for drugs coming in from Mexico. Just *great!* And here I was right in the midst of all of it. . . .

"Want a joint?" I turned from Yancy to look up into the outstretched hand of a guy I had never seen before. They were passing the stuff, and it was my turn to take a hit.

"No thanks," I answered, and turned back to resume my conversation.

"What's wrong, baby? Don't you like our stuff?" He thrust the cigarette closer to me.

"No, thank you—I just don't smoke—anything." I was frightened and wanted to be anywhere in the world but in Tyler's garage. Then Yancy was on his feet, moving my intruder in the opposite direction.

"Hey, man, the lady doesn't *need* it. Don't you wish you didn't, either?" Instantly Yancy was beside me again, and the incident, I'm sure, was lost from his memory. But not from mine! I will never forget the pride I felt for him that night. Yancy had a new strength about him that I had never seen before, but I had always believed it was there. He might make it, after all!

On New Year's Eve Yancy's mom was giving a party in my honor, and I knew that it was "then or never." I could offer Yancy anything that any other woman could and I was determined to prove it to him. I was going to fight for what I loved, even if it meant a compromise of all I had been taught and believed. Somehow it all seemed worth it.

Purple Passion Punch got the evening started in a big way. By midnight I was on Yancy's lap toasting 1971. I hadn't indulged in the punch for fear of not knowing what was happening when the moment arrived.

Shortly after the twelve o'clock chaos, Yancy and I went into his room to "talk." I'll never forget the wild emotion in my being as we began to "discuss" our future. I should have known that our future was sabotaged from the very beginning.

"Yancy!" his mother cried as she rushed through the door and shocked us into reality. "Don't you do anything you'll be sorry for!"

Suddenly my senses returned, and I sat up and rear-ranged my clothing. "Doesn't she know what kind of girl I am?" I asked indignantly.

Yancy shook his head in disbelief and took my hands in his. "She knows, Kathryn, and she wants you to stay that way. And I do, too. Go on to bed, I'll see you in the morning."

Thanks a lot, Lord!

3

New Direction

Don't let anyone think little of you because you are young. Be their ideal; let them follow the way you teach and live; be a pattern for them in your love, your faith, and your clean thoughts.

1 Timothy 4:12

Looking back now I realize that it was only Christ's strength that got me through those next six months. It was sort of like a six-month supply of vitamin C. Pensacola was behind me now; and, at times, it seemed like I had only been dreaming the whole thing. Soon I would awaken from the nightmare.

I couldn't bear the thought of Yancy with another woman, too far away for me to convince him that he loved *me!* I can't explain how I knew that he did, I just knew. "O God, please don't let him marry her," I whispered nightly into my pillow. "I'll do anything if You'll only work a miracle and save Yancy from her. . . ." What a fool I was to think that Yancy needed to be saved from the grips of a woman. He needed to be saved from the grips of *sin—*

he needed *salvation* through Jesus! Finally that fact reached my brain—a long, stubborn way at times!

I began to gear all my energies toward prayer for Yancy's salvation. I fasted. I spent long dark hours in tearful communion with God. And I waited daily for word from Yancy; only for the first time, it never came. Then one day, late in January, I got a letter from Yancy's sister. Yancy and Pam were getting married in April! Numbness embraced my body as I read those words. In that one moment I lost all desire to live. I know what it is like to lose someone so dear to you that you might as well have lost your own life.

I climbed the stairs to my bedroom, clutching the letter in my hand. I fell to the floor, crushing beneath me the seashells Yancy and I had collected on New Year's Day. I felt deserted—abandoned. But I could forgive Yancy as I had so many times in the past. It was God I could not forgive. I had trusted Him, waited on Him, and believed that He would work a miracle. Now here was my miracle: Yancy was going to marry Pam. It was the thought that Jesus had forsaken me that caused me to bash my head repeatedly against the solid wall. I fell to the floor, reeling from the pain and the greater agony of not even being able to kill myself. *Couldn't I do anything right?*

As you have obviously surmised, I did not succeed in killing myself on that cold and dark January day. Instead, I existed day by day in a living death. I don't know which state is worse. Gone was my smiling optimism, my child-like faith, my instant laughter. The old Kathie was dead and the new one wished she were, too.

I went through those days completely oblivious to the world around me. It is nothing short of a miracle that I won first place in the Maryland Junior Miss Pageant. I captured the poise and appearance, physical fitness, judges' interview, and talent categories as well. The crown of laurel leaves slipped from my head and rested on my nose as I walked down the victory runway. It was a perfect symbol of the way I felt. All I could think of was how disappointed Yancy would be that I had won my ego trip. Some victory.

My family was once again racked with sorrow. No one knew how to handle the situation, for the slightest provocation would set me off in a flood of tears.

Healing for this kind of malady can only come from the inside out. You have to want to be delivered, want to be something better than you are. You can't help someone who doesn't want to be healed. For a long time it was impossible to help me because I was happy being miserable. But then, gradually, I began to let Jesus help me smile again—just a little at first. Soon it came more easily; finally I even began to laugh a bit.

"What famous person would you like to spend an hour with?" I was sitting at the kitchen table filling out my questionnaire for the national Junior Miss Pageant and got excited when I finally found a question I could answer easily. Anita Bryant came to my mind immediately; after all, I'd been praying for her for years and I felt like I already knew her.

"Kathie, you must pray for Anita Bryant and Vonda Kay Van Dyke. They are Christians in a world where it's extra

hard to be one—show business." The very idea had cap-
tivated me since my mother first spoke of it, so I faithfully
began to lift up these two women in prayer. This was long
before Anita became the Florida Sunshine Lady!

Soon after I had sent in all my forms to Mobile, Alabama, the traditional site of the national pageant, I read
in the Junior Miss newsletter that Anita Bryant would
cohost the contest along with Ed McMahon, of "Tonight
Show" fame. Something in me, even then, told me that I
would be having more than a casual chat with this talented lady—and for once, I was right!

I'll never forget the first time I saw her. All the girls
from the fifty states were rehearsing in the giant auditorium when Anita walked in with her husband-manager,
Bob Green. "Have you had your *orange juice* today?" she
jokingly questioned one of the girls. The poor girl who was
so shaken by the sudden attention could only nod affirma-
tively.

"Good!" Anita laughed. "My work is not in vain!" We
loved her instantly. Throughout the pageant she took care
to speak to each girl individually, inquiring about families
and homes. She even held an autographing session for us,
signing her new book *Mine Eyes Have Seen the Glory*—
no small chore at fifty books! And always her husband was
at her side.

Bob Green intrigued me almost more than Anita did.
She was so open and warm; yet there was a silent strength
about Bob, forever checking and rechecking the many
details which I felt sure had helped to bring Anita to her
present professional stature. Behind this great woman

there had to be a great man! I was anxious to get to know Bob Green, the person, not just Bob, Anita Bryant's husband.

By now I was well into my ten-day stay in Mobile. I was already convinced that Junior Miss is one of the greatest growing experiences that a young girl can have. Never before had I been so challenged to be my own person— to think my own thoughts—and be proud of what I was as a completely unique individual. The greatest miracle of all was that I discovered I had a real gift to sing. I had prepared "Go Down, Moses," an old Negro spiritual, as my talent presentation. But even after winning both the Bowie and Maryland talent awards I was still not convinced of my musical ability. So I had written a poem about slavery which I recited in dramatic form before I sang the song—just in case!

Anita told me later that it was my voice that first attracted her and Bob to me. They had just entered the auditorium one day during a talent rehearsal and were standing outside the stage doors when Anita was taken by a voice from within the hall. "Bob," she exclaimed, "they finally got a black girl in the pageant!" They opened the door and got their first look at me—whiter than a whitewashed fence.

Losing the top title in the Junior Miss Pageant was one of the greatest victories I have ever known! Only Jesus can turn what seems to be a defeat into a real asset in your life. I know I had performed well throughout the preliminaries. My voice was strong, my brother had seen to it that I was more than physically fit, and my attitude was great.

A lot of people picked me as the winner, and I really thought I would win. *What better way to be a witness for the Lord? Surely this was what He had had in mind for me all along!* How guilty we all are at times of "deciding" God's plan for us!

For, you see, I did win. I gained a new poise, a deeper self-confidence, and a greater commitment to start my life all over again with Jesus, instead of Yancy, at my side. April 30 was the date of my judge's interview, the most important scoring category of the pageant. It was also Yancy's wedding day. All of the security I had felt so strongly throughout the week melted from me like ice cream on a sunny day. Once again I was the jittery, timid, frightened Kathie I had so recently been. Like a fool I cried during my interview. I just couldn't help myself. How could a loving God let Yancy get married less than fifty miles away on a day when more than ever I needed to be strong?

God doesn't answer questions like that. He asks, instead, that you wait it out and trust Him for the final good of it. It seemed too cruel a request. I left the interview knowing that I had not impressed the judges with my ability to be America's Junior Miss. I doubted it, too.

The Kraft Hostess Award, given annually by Kraft Foods, a national sponsor, is one of the biggest prizes in the pageant. Prior to coming to Mobile each girl has to plan an entire party, complete with invitations, menu, decorations, and games. This reflects her creativity and ingenuity, not to mention her ability to use Kraft products in her recipes! Her entry is then sent to Chicago for judging by a special panel of experts.

I really enjoyed this aspect of the competition. I love to work with my hands, love to cook, and love to have parties, so I threw all my creative energies into my "Hang Ten" luau. It was intended to be a welcome-back party for my Pensacola friends; and it must have expressed every ounce of love I have for them because I won first place— a $1500 scholarship and a contract to film a Kraft commercial. You can imagine my excitement at finally winning something other than a good lesson in life! I just had to share my excitement with someone, but my folks were away on a sight-seeing tour with the rest of the parents and couldn't be reached. I had to tell *somebody!* My impatience caused me to make the final fatal mistake.

I noticed a guy I had become friendly with earlier in the week, so I ran over to share my news with him. I didn't stop to think that it was against pageant rules to talk to boys—in fact, I didn't even know it—but by then the damage was done. The judges witnessed my unfortunate outburst and made note of it in their folders. I was doomed! But by then it didn't even matter.

The final night of the pageant was to be televised nationally by NBC, and the air was tingling with excitement and good-natured teasing. "Remember me when you're rich and famous, Kentucky!" "Kneel, Wisconsin, when in the presence of your queen!" All the girls were relieved that it would soon be over and they would be free to go home to their boyfriends and senior proms. I've never experienced such goodwill among girls in a competitive situation. I really think it had much to do with the high caliber of the girls who represented, with poise and pride, the states whose names they bore. Twenty-three of the fifty girls professed to being reborn Christians!

Right before air time I found myself backstage talking with Bob Green and several of the other Junior Misses.

"What are you going to do now?" Bob asked me in his famously nonchalant manner. "You planning on college in the fall?"

I had to admit that the idea was very unappealing. "No, I really don't want to go to school right away. I'd like to work somewhere for a year before I do—maybe Disney World."

Bob looked interested. "Yeah? Well, maybe Anita and I can help you, we've got a lot of friends at Disney. You could probably start this summer."

"I'd really appreciate that!" I said excitedly. "Except it will have to be after June. I'm going to Israel with my mother for the Jerusalem Conference on Biblical Prophecy, but after that. . . ."

"You are?" Bob couldn't have unnerved me more! "Come with me, come on, we've got to tell Anita!" He proceeded to rush me toward Anita's dressing room, much to the delight and amusement of my Junior Miss buddies.

Anita zipped up hurriedly as Bob barged through the door with me trailing right behind in utter confusion.

"Anita!" he exclaimed, "The Lord has answered our prayers!" At this both Anita and I looked at Bob in puzzled amazement.

"We've got a *baby-sitter!*"

4

"Gews and Jentiles"

But I will court her again, and bring her into the wilderness, and speak to her tenderly there. There I will give back her vineyards to her, and transform her Valley of Troubles into a Door of Hope. She will respond to me there, singing with joy as in the days long ago in her youth. . . .

Hosea 2:14–15

I had always hated my last name—*Epstein.* Sheer poetry, isn't it? Maybe my disgust had something to do with my wanting to get married so young—any last name would be better than Epstein! But I have changed my mind completely now. I'm grateful for my Jewish heritage. The Bible says that salvation came to the world through the Jews (*see* John 4:22).

Never have I experienced the nature of my Jewishness as I did while in the Holy Land. The whole Bible came alive for me as I walked along the ancient roads that Jesus Himself had traveled so often and knew so well. Time was suspended. At night I even snuggled close to my pillow for fear that Moses might be standing beside the bed if I opened my eyes.

But I *loved* it! I loved every inch of the country, the zeal of the people for their homeland, and the great reverence for their rich history. Our pilgrimages to the familiar biblical sites gave me a new respect for the past which I continue to cherish.

My mother was in a dream world and didn't want to wake up. She arose long before the rest of us so that she would not miss even one jewel of delight Israel could offer her. Mom trudged on tirelessly (in 113 degree heat) throughout the ruins of Jericho and Caesarea. She made me feel like an old lady! I couldn't help but giggle at her schoolgirl awe of the land around her. I truly believe that she got more of a blessing out of that trip than anyone else on the tour. She's just that kind of person who accepts a gift, no matter how small, with the greatest appreciation.

Mom is as gentile as you can get. Her blonde hair and beautiful blue eyes looked amusingly foreign in a country where dark hair and even darker eyes dominate the population. The Jewish part of my lineage comes unmistakably from my father's side of the family. My daddy's father was a Russian Jew who immigrated to America many years ago and married a gentile, my grandmother. Although he attended the Episcopalian church, the Jewish traditions were still very much a part of my father's childhood. When he and my mother were married the influence remained—bagels were a way of life for me! I felt uniquely comfortable in this exotic land that cradles the past and the future within its tiny boundaries.

We had been in Israel for several days, and I had not yet heard a word from Anita and Bob. One day I found a message from them at my hotel desk: Mom and I were invited to Bob's fortieth birthday party that night at the Gondola, a fabulous Italian restaurant right in the heart of Old Jerusalem!

It was a great celebration. Mom and I joined Gloria Roe and her husband, Ron Robertson, Charlie and Marabel Morgan, and Bobby and Gloria Green to complete the guest list. I adored the children from the very start, although I must admit that they were a little bewildered by my presence there that night! Many times since then I have thought fondly of that quaint little restaurant on King George Street and wanted to return. I hope it never changes!

Bobby and Gloria and I became terrific buddies during the remainder of the trip. We visited landmarks and went shopping in the colorful bazaars. Sometimes we just stayed in the hotel and watched TV or played games together. I was surprised at their naturalness, their unaffected acceptance of their famous mother. Sure, they had all the material things they needed in this world, but still their spirits were pure and their hearts were really hungry to know more about Jesus. They were hardly spoiled brats!

Bob and Anita were more than generous to me. Before our visit together was over, I was presented with a sterling silver crusaders' cross as payment for my baby-sitting services. All this, and it had even been fun!

Israel speeded the healing process of losing Yancy. I

desperately needed to be away from all the familiar sights and sounds, and my trip to the Holy Land the summer of 1971 was the perfect diversion.

Standing in front of the Garden Tomb, the site believed to be the authentic burial place of Jesus after His Crucifixion, I gained a deeper insight into, ironically enough, life. I suddenly realized that what is really important is the state of a person's soul. I had experienced this same profound enlightenment only once, three years before, when my brother was missing in California for three days.

David had traveled to San Francisco to "find himself" and was robbed of every cent he had the very first night he was there. Too proud to call home for help, he ditched his luggage and hitchhiked down the coast to San Diego where he enlisted in the Marines. However, we knew none of this. Only his luggage was found in a Santa Cruz bus terminal, and the police notified us in Maryland of his disappearance. My family fasted and prayed during those terrible three days and nights while we waited for news of him.

David didn't know Jesus as his Saviour. He battled intellectually with the biblical professions, but could not be convinced of their truth. He was a prolific reader, and this obsession only served to intensify his already confused state of mind. David would read one classic right after the next, finding bits of truth within each, but never enough to convince him entirely. Then, like a giant jigsaw puzzle, he would try to fit the treasured pieces into one grand philosophical *truth*. He became more discouraged and frustrated with each book he read, so he decided to travel to California and find *truth* for himself. He found it, alright. The painfully ugly truth of poverty, muggers in the night, and spiritual emptiness. David had entered the cultural revolution and discovered that it was much more attractive from the outside looking in. The very sad thing is that so few young people are lucky enough to emerge triumphantly from their battles with the revolution as David did. His search for meaning ended in a corn patch one night as he knelt and invited Christ to take over his life. His spirit was exhausted! He could no longer run from the real Truth, Jesus.

Now as I knelt inside the dark, damp tomb I reexperienced those emotions I'd had three years before. I hadn't known if David was dead, without Christ, or was alive somewhere in a living hell. I realized that lost souls are what really matter after all. I couldn't utter a sound, there alone with Mom with such holy ground beneath us. We both began to cry for joy! Jesus had conquered it all for us! A new surge of faith swelled inside me. God had heard my prayers and had saved my brother into His Kingdom. Surely He would do the same for Yancy! But in His timing, and in His own way. It was finally out of my hands. Jesus had already accomplished it, for me, for David, for Yancy, and for you, two thousand years ago, right there where I knelt.

5

A Lemon in Orange Juice

My soul claims the Lord as my inheritance; therefore I will hope in him. It is good both to hope and wait quietly for the salvation of the Lord.

Lamentations 3:24, 26

Israel, Greece, and Italy were all tucked neatly away in my memory. I was home in Delaware at our beach house to spend the summer months before starting college in the fall. In spite of my desire to forego school for a year, I had somehow succumbed to the social pressure of following the inevitable educational route. That way you avoid having to make excuses as to why "an *A* student like you" isn't in college!

Mom and I were so glad to be home. It had been a terrific trip, but an exhausting one, too. Now we were looking forward to a relaxing vacation in Rehoboth Beach where we had spent the five previous summers; it is a picturesque little city by the Atlantic Ocean, famous only for a rickety old boardwalk that creaks under your bicycle wheels. It was my special place, for it was there that I met and fell in love with Yancy.

I knew it would be a difficult summer, having to face all the familiar places and faces without him for the first time. I never dreamed Yancy would show up and complicate the situation even more!

I saw him one night soon after I had returned from Israel. He was sitting with Pam on a bench in the middle of the village square. Everything in me wanted to turn around and run from the encounter I knew was inevitable. But I gathered every bit of courage I could muster and whispered a prayer for strength as I slowly walked towards them. "Hi, Yancy," I said softly. "Hello, Pam."

"Hello, Kathryn. I'm glad to see you," Yancy said as I avoided his eyes meeting mine. "How was your trip?"

I began to share my experiences in the Holy Land, trying to hurry so that I could escape from the discomfort and the embarrassment and the terrible feeling in the pit of my stomach. But as I started to describe the Garden Tomb, once again the same emotions rose within me and I cried unashamedly from the joy I had found there only a week before. Finally I looked up, and Yancy was weeping too.

"I believe, Kathryn. I accepted Jesus into my heart two weeks ago and now I believe."

His words were so long awaited that I hardly dreamed they were true. And yet, they were! Yancy was saved, he believed! Still in a haze from the shock of his words, I barely heard him tell me that Pam, too, had asked Christ into her life at Rock Church in Virginia Beach.

In that one moment it was all worth it. I felt like a

mother must feel when her child is finally born into the world. All the pain is forgotten in one instant as she looks upon the miracle of her baby's birth. It all seemed so easy now, well worth the weight of a human soul. Thank You, Lord Jesus, for using me in some small way to aid Your Kingdom. It hit me right then that Jesus actually loved Yancy even more than I did. Impossible, but true!

The rest of the summer was spent in the joys of Christian fellowship. Bible studies, communion services, and song fests were daily fare. I knew that it was only a matter of time before others would catch on to the fire that Yancy had lit. For years I had warned Yancy of his responsibility as a leader to use his influence for the good of those who followed him. "Yancy, one of these days you're going to use your power for some good. You're going to lead all your friends to the Lord instead of the ocean." As usual, he would just smile and say, "For sure." It seemed incredible at the time, yet now it was a wonderful reality!

One by one Yancy's buddies accepted Jesus Christ as their Lord and Saviour and began a new life in service to Him. And they all agreed that there was no high like the high of being *saved!*

The days went by and I made plans to enter a Florida university in September. Just one day before I was supposed to send in my registration fee for the fall semester, I received a long-distance telephone call from Miami. As I accepted the receiver from my father, I sat down for what I knew would be an important conversation.

"Is this Kathie Epstein?" a deep voice asked.

"Yes," I answered hesitantly.

"Is this *the* Kathie Epstein?"

By now I was laughing at Anita and Bob, calling me *the anybody!* Excited anticipation welled up inside me as I listened to their proposition. "Kathie, we've been fighting it for five days and we just can't get it off our minds that we're supposed to ask you to come and live with us," Anita said. "The Lord just hasn't given us a minute's peace, so what do you say?"

What *could* I say? "When do you want me to come?" I asked, signaling my folks to keep quiet.

"Can you come tomorrow?" Anita laughed.

Panic struck me. "Well, can I turn eighteen first?" I asked, still trying to hush my family.

"How soon can you do that? We want you to come as quickly as you can."

I did some fast figuring and answered, "My birthday is in two weeks; I guess I could come right after that." I hardly knew what I was saying. I hung up the receiver and faced my anxious family in total disbelief. *What next?*

So I turned eighteen as fast I could and, three days later, was in Miami Beach taking up residence at Villa Verde with the Bob Green family. As I drove from the airport I couldn't help but remember the final night of the Junior Miss Pageant in Mobile. When the winner was announced, crowds of people engulfed an exuberant Miss New Jersey with congratulations. I, too, was on my way to join the well-wishers when Anita came directly toward me and said, "Praise the Lord, Kathie!"

"I do, Miss Bryant," I answered her, not a little embarrassed at the sudden attention.

"Just think," she said, "if you had won, we might never have had the chance to get to know each other!" And now I was only minutes away from being a permanent member of the household.

I must admit I was absolutely unprepared for everything that greeted me behind those Spanish walls at Villa Verde. I have never been a great typist; as a matter of fact, I typed in the "seek and ye shall find" method that completely infuriated my high-school typing teacher. And yet now I was to be Bob's secretary as well as Anita's personal secretary! You can believe I did some heavy praying!

My first three months with the Greens were *traumatic,* to put it mildly. Not only was it the first time I'd been away from my family and friends, it was also the first time I had been entrusted with so many professional responsibilities. It scared me to death! Hotel reservations, correspondence, filings (Have you any idea how many magazine and newspaper articles that woman has been featured in?), personal-appearance bookings, and airline routings just began the list of my daily chores. Invariably the telephone would interrupt me at the most crucial moments. How I longed for the peace and quiet of college life!

The children became my one great joy. I had grown close to Bobby and Gloria while we were in Israel; but the twins, Barbara and Billy, greeted me upon my arrival in Miami. I knew at once that I had never seen more beautiful babies in my life—hardly like the weak and sickly infants who were born prematurely only two and a half years earlier. They were truly "miracle" babies, perfect little dolls filled with more energy than a whole bottle of vitamins! It wasn't long before I was dubbed "Kaffy Kake," and they became the "Green Beans."

So that is the story of how I came to a new home and a new life in Florida. My environment was picture-post-card perfect: a beautiful villa on Biscayne Bay and my own luxurious apartment complete with the choicest food and two television sets. But I was lonely. Bob and Anita did all they could to make me comfortable; however, the life-style was such a drastic change from the one I had always known that it became increasingly more difficult for me to find contentment. I was busier than I had ever been, but all too soon it became an empty busyness. I didn't want the Greens to think that I was ungrateful, so for several months I smiled all day and cried all night, alone in my apartment. "What's wrong with me, Lord?" I kept asking Him, "I know You brought me here for a reason, but I'm going to lose my mind unless You reveal it to me. If You want me to work all day in the office and go to school at night and take care of the kids on the weekends, then You are just going to have to give me the desire for it. I can't make it without You."

The fire that kept me going, when I thought I could go no further, was that Bob and Anita wanted to help me with my singing career. They had spent ten years looking for someone they could guide along in a professional career, sharing all of their knowledge and experience. They felt that the Lord had brought me into their lives for this purpose, so Bob began telling pastors and youth leaders about me when they called to book Anita. Naturally, I wasn't their first choice, but Bob's recommendation satisfied any doubts they might have had. I was booked, and I was terrified!

My first engagement was held in Tampa, Florida. I was to sing and give my testimony before several thousand young Baptists assembled there in a great auditorium. I remember perfectly my conversation with God that day: "Lord, what am I going to say? I don't have any fantastic testimony—I was never into drugs or sex or anything else that people like to hear about. I'm just a nobody with nothing to say."

"You know Me in a personal way, don't you?" He asked me.

"Yes."

"Well then, you've got something to say!" And of course, He was right. Every Christian has something important to share because Jesus has dealt with each of us in a completely private and personal way. We each have a story that no one else can tell, for no two salvation accounts are just alike. God cares about us enough to speak to us individually, uniquely. I couldn't love a God who didn't!

If I had not told my story that day, hearts would not have been opened to the living Christ. If you don't tell your story, whether it is because you are afraid or insecure, someone will not hear the Gospel of Jesus. The Bible tells us that we are to give an account of the hope that is within us. It doesn't have to be in front of multitudes—only some are called to that—but it must be to that one person that the Lord will bring your way today. If we are not faithful with a little, how can He entrust us with much?

I stood trembling and perspiring before that great crowd—it looked like fifty thousand to me! I was so grateful for the podium I was leaning against—it concealed my knees as they knocked together in fear! But I discovered that day that the will of God will never lead me where the grace of God will not keep me.

I simply shared from my heart and loved those kids with my eyes and smile. I sang only to Jesus, they just happened to be there listening. They got the message. I couldn't believe that they were on their feet, applauding as I stood there with tears streaming down my cheeks. They were really clapping for the Lord, Himself. I was just privileged to be a willing vessel of His love.

6

Come On and Take a Free Ride

I don't want your sacrifices—I want your love; I don't want your offerings—I want you to know me.

Hosea 6:6

I love the story of Mary and Martha in the Bible. They were entertaining Jesus in their home, and Martha was scurrying around preparing the meal and busying herself with the tiniest detail. But Mary sat at the Master's feet and listened to His words, worshiped Him with her attention, and adored Him with her eyes. It was Mary whom Jesus commended, setting her as an example of how we could please Him.

I was a perfect Martha those last few months with the Green family. I became so busy working for the Lord that I forgot who I was working *for!* I gave up my night classes at the local junior college so that I could be free to accept the invitations which, by now, I was receiving in great abundance. I did a lot of traveling, often going as far as Texas and Kansas to do concerts. I expanded my repertoire so that I could easily do one-and-a-half-hour banquets. Bob and I designed a publicity kit that we sent all over the country. It was complete with pictures and newspaper and magazine articles. We made plans to record an album and write a book. Busy, yes. But busy for whom?

As active as Anita was, I noticed that she never neglected her private time with the Lord. She had a fire for the Word that put my little flicker to shame. I longed to have that kind of hunger in my heart—but not enough to do anything about it!

Anita and I were sitting in the breakfast room one morning having coffee and going over some of her mail. "This person wants to know why you're such a fanatic!" I laughed, handing her the letter.

She became so still I thought she was going to be faint. A faraway look came across her face and she said sadly, "I wish I were a fanatic, Kathie, then I'd be *totally* sold out to Jesus."

I had always respected Anita Bryant as a great human being, but never really thought critically about her as a performer. All it took was one exposure to her "live" show to make a believer out of me for life. Anita has that rare ability to make the audience eat right out of her hand. They love her. They love her because she gives every bit of herself to them for those forty minutes she's on the stage. By the time the last note of the "Battle Hymn of the Republic" is triumphantly sung, all of the people in the room are on their feet cheering one of America's finest artists.

Needless to say, I've learned a lot from Anita. I must have seen her show a hundred times, but each new performance taught me something fresh and exciting. One habit of Anita's I hope I never pick up is her passion for hot-fudge sundaes after the show. Her svelte little figure can handle it, but I'd eat it today and wear it tomorrow!

At first I was really thrilled and flattered at being compared so often with Anita. I mean, I could do worse, right? Then one night after a performance I overheard two elderly ladies discussing my program: "She's another Anita Bryant, you know!"

That was the beginning of my "identity crisis." I suddenly became keenly aware that I was not developing my own personal potential. I was not becoming the woman God wanted me to be. Instead I was painting a reproduction of an original. Reproductions aren't bad, but they sure ain't the real thing! I struggled to free myself from the web I had spun, but the threads were already too tight. So rather than handling the situation maturely and talking it out with Anita and Bob, I held all the frustration inside me and began to resent all the sincere compliments which were given to me in total innocence. It was easier than facing the real problems—my own feelings of inadequacy as a person and as a performer. I began to see Anita as the source of all the conflict; it was because of my close relationship with her that I was unable to grow into my own person and find myself spiritually, emotionally, and musically. Even if I didn't like what I found, at least I would have the assurance of knowing that it was the real me! Every human being needs that satisfaction. They need to know that they have either achieved or failed to achieve on the basis of personal merits alone.

I know this hurt Anita and Bob deeply. They had come to love me as their own daughter and their desire to help me professionally was soon overshadowed by their efforts to shield me from all of the heartache of the big, bad world of show business. They didn't understand my impatience, my passion to have things yesterday instead of tomorrow. I suppose I frightened Anita because she saw so much of herself in me, and she couldn't bear the thought of my having to experience the pitfalls which she knew only too well.

The last thing I wanted then was another mother! I felt like life was passing me by and my youth would be gone in the morning. I wanted to use it while I still had it and could still relate to my "lost" generation. When I was sixteen I hardly even communicated with anyone over twenty-one, and yet now I was swiftly approaching that dreaded age myself! In all of my struggling I just couldn't see that God was trying to mold me into that woman He had designed me to be. He can use mature people who walk in the Spirit and trust Him day by day, but it's hard to bear fruit from a vine that is determined to be free of its roots.

The mind has a way of distorting a situation and exaggerating it out of proportion. My mind convinced me that I needed to leave Miami, needed to leave Anita and Bob, and needed to leave all the security they could offer me. I had to learn my lesson all over again: until you submit to His will and yield to His direction, you struggle against a brick wall. He cannot lead you when you are fighting against Him. So once again I began to praise God in all things.

"Then trust Me!"

"Yes, Lord," I answered, "only You're going to have to do it all because it's going to take a *miracle!*" That's all He wanted to hear. . . .

The next morning I woke up with the Voice still ringing in my ears: "I love Jesus, Jesus loves me. What others pay for, I'll get free." I couldn't make any sense out of it in the daylight, either!

Several days passed and I began to wonder if I had been dreaming after all. But then Kurt Kaiser, the wonderful Christian composer and arranger, came to visit the camp and he took me aside to give me a little advice.

"Kathie, you have a fine talent," he stated, "a fine singing voice that you should use for the Lord. If I were you, I'd go away for a while—to school maybe—and find myself musically. You sound too much like Anita!"

There it was again and it was like a confirmation from God that He was working things out. Still I doubted!

Camp finally ended and we moved the hundred miles back to Miami Beach. I was sitting in the office one morning, catching up on the piles of accumulated work, when Anita threw open the door and stood there facing me with tears in her eyes.

"Kathie, I just talked to Oral."

"Oral who?" I asked, not being at all familiar with that name.

"Oral Roberts. He says you can come out to his college in Tulsa, and they'll make all of the arrangements for your admission. You start in two weeks!"

7

O.R.U. Happy?

Yet there is one ray of hope: his compassion never ends.
It is only the Lord's mercies that have kept us from com-
plete destruction. Great is his faithfulness; his loving-
kindness begins afresh each day.

Lamentations 3:21–23

I had a million things to do: so many people to see one
more time, and so much unfinished business to be com-
pleted. I was in a state of shock, my body was going
through all the motions with a totally unattached brain!
By now I was remarkably accustomed to this crazy way of
life. I noticed a pattern: the Lord always gave me two
weeks before He transplanted me clear across the country! I began to wonder, *Did this have anything to do with
my persistent independence in running the affairs of my
life?*

I came down to the kitchen on the morning of my last
day at Villa Verde. Anita had called me while I was pack-
ing in my apartment and had bluntly commanded me to
come immediately to the breakfast room. Her tone fright-

ened me! She sounded disturbed, and the last thing I wanted to do was leave on a sour note!

"Surprise!" the children screamed as I walked into the room which was decorated for a party and full of presents.

"We'll all miss you, Kaffy Kake," Anita said, trying not to show that she was close to tears. "We just wanted to show you how much we love you."

I managed to remain poised; that is, until Anita handed me one of her famous gold fishhooks—even bigger than the one she gave to Billy Graham—and said, "Fish for Jesus, honey." At that I buried my head in her shoulder and let it all go!

I felt a strange emptiness as Michie and I looked down from the airplane window at the city that had been my home for a year now. Fear swept through me—the fear that always comes from making a decision and then wondering if you've made a mistake. But this time I knew that God Himself had made the decision for me. I had two families now, one in Maryland and one in Florida. Soon I would be alone once again, this time in a city I had never visited, at a school that was little more to me than a name! Yet I knew the Lord would make a home for me, and it would be filled with people who loved me. It was only a matter of time!

Michie and I spent those next two weeks in Rehoboth Beach. I was out shopping for school clothes one afternoon when a long-distance phone call came for me from Washington, D.C. My father answered the phone and, being the lovingly protective parent that he is, demanded to know who was calling.

"The White House," came the reply. My father quietly returned the receiver to its cradle, thinking it was a prank call! Later the phone rang again and, not knowing of Daddy's earlier action, I answered it myself.

"Is this Miss Kathie Epstein?" a young voice asked. I convinced him that he had the right number, and he proceeded to tell me that he was an aide to the President and was calling to invite me to be a guest soloist at the Republican National Convention!

Surely there was some mistake! The White House couldn't possibly want *me* . . . there must be another Kathie Epstein somewhere that. . . .

"Fine, then we'll see you in Miami Beach, Miss Epstein." I hung up and sat there in dumb amazement. I was going back to Miami Beach long before I had expected, on a mission I never imagined possible!

I was already committed to a crusade in Ocala, Florida, but the Lord provided a way for me to fly to Miami, sing at the convention, and be back in Ocala a few hours later for the evening service. A member of the church I was visiting owned a private plane; together we flew through the night, pounded and slashed about by a terrible summer storm. I had little rest that night! Over and over I whispered, "The joy of the Lord is my strength!" (*See* Nehemiah 8:10.) I prayed that the Lord would uphold me physically and anoint me spiritually to glorify Him when the moment finally arrived.

I was to sing one hymn, "Amazing Grace," at the beginning of the hour-long opening worship service of the convention. All of the participants met prior to the service for coffee and fellowship in a room adjoining the main auditorium. I felt like a little peon in the midst of such famous faces. I looked around in awe, then trembled as I was introduced to: Frank Borman, the astronaut; Senator John Tower of Texas; George Romney, then Secretary of Health, Education, and Welfare; Jimmy MacDonald, the marvelous gospel singer; and Cliff Barrows, of Billy Graham Crusade fame. Not only was I unknown, I was the only woman, too!

I needed prayer desperately. I noticed Mr. Barrows standing off to the left of me, so I walked over to ask him to pray that the Lord would minister His love through me. I didn't mean right there, right out loud! But there we stood in the middle of the room, Cliff Barrows holding both my hands in his as he prayed one of the most beautiful prayers in my behalf I have ever heard:

Lord God, thank You for my sister, Kathie. Thank You for her talent that she has dedicated to You. You brought her here, Lord, to be an instrument of Your love. I pray that right now You will cast aside all fear and give her Your peace within, so that she can sing as she's never sung before, Lord. For You. In Christ's Name I pray, Amen.

Needless to say, I have been madly in love with Cliff Barrows ever since!

I did sing that Sunday morning as I never had before. Once again, as in Tampa, I took my eyes off the VIPs and their families in the front rows and I sang for Jesus, and

His Amazing Grace!

One week later I was in Tulsa, Oklahoma, a freshman at Oral Roberts University. O.R.U. is not a school that you can easily describe, it must be experienced. It is a family, an education, and a fellowship all rolled into one five-hundred-acre campus in the heart of America's green country. However, O.R.U. is not the modern buildings or the television shows or the lush land on which it sits. Oral Roberts University is the *spirit* of the people who live there. Because the people are not perfect, neither is O.R.U.; but there is an atmosphere of striving to be the whole person in body, mind, and soul. That's what makes it unforgettable.

At first I had a great deal of difficulty being "young" again. I hadn't dated during my year in Miami, and the only young people I had been in contact with were those I spoke before or sang to in a guest situation. I was determined to keep as much of my recent past as secret as possible.

I realize now that this sudden fear of revealing my past was related to similar fears I had known before, even the reluctance about my last name. I just wasn't happy about being *me*. I didn't like myself, and consequently I had trouble believing that God did, much less others.

I hadn't been at O.R.U. more than a month when the truth came out, as it always does. President Roberts asked if I would sing in chapel at a special service in honor of Governor George Wallace. The Governor of Alabama had received severe gunshot wounds the previous spring during a political rally at a Maryland shopping center. He had requested prayer from the O.R.U. faculty and student body. I am from Bowie, Maryland, a town only a few miles away from the site of the shooting, so President Roberts thought it would be particularly appropriate for me to sing and pray for him over the special telephone hookup we had established with Governor Wallace's mansion in Birmingham. Naturally I was honored, but I was also a bit more nervous than usual at appearing before the student body for the first time. I was not prepared for President Roberts's introductory speech; before I knew it, he had shared the details of my admission to the school a month earlier. My heart sank as the shadow of secrecy slipped away from me. Suddenly I felt naked and alone, a slave to all I had been and could not escape from still being.

I learned a valuable lesson that day: I am who I am. I am what I am because of who I was yesterday and all that I have experienced until today. Even if we want to, we cannot conceal the past—good or bad—for the past lives on boldly in our present selves. The only way to be free of yesterday's burdens is to bravely face them in the light of today. Accept your past in any way that you must in order to justify its presence in your life right now. Only then will you be truly ready to face tomorrow. Remember that Jesus not only forgives, He also *forgets!*

I have found that *praise* is the surest route to peace of mind. I do not regret what has happened before, I now thank God for it. I do not understand many things about it; but neither do I understand electricity, yet I accept its reality because I have seen the evidence of its existence. In the same way I have seen the evidence of God's existence in my life, working through my experiences as He shapes me for the future. If God were small enough for my mind, He certainly would not be big enough for my needs.

God is like a product you've been using for a long time that really satisfies you—it does the job again and again and never lets you down. Every once in a while a new product comes on the market that tempts you to switch; it's flashier, and it offers a whole new set of promises. You may even try it for a time, until you realize it's a far cry from the wonder worker you expected! If you're like me, you hurry back to your original product, more convinced than ever of its quality and a lot less likely to switch again.

God did not disappoint me or let me down with Yancy, or with Junior Miss, or with my life in Miami, either. God has the greatest record of success you can find anywhere! Why stop trusting Him now?

Yancy is a perfect example of how guilt over the past can seriously affect achievement in the present. Yancy suffered a great deal over his past after he accepted the Lord. He knew Jesus forgave him, but he just couldn't forgive himself. One day he approached his pastor with his problem. His pastor sat him down and reassured him with this contemporary parable.

Yancy, pretend it's Judgement Day and it's your turn to come up before the Lord. You stand there trembling and frightened and, when God asks you your name, you can barely whisper it—you're so scared.

"Yancy, huh?" God says as He thumbs through the

pages of the Book of Life. "Yes, your name is in here —come on in, son. Enter into the joy of your Lord!"

"But, Lord," you say, "what about the time I cursed Your name?"

"Hey, I don't remember that, but I'll look. No, there's nothing here about that. Come on in!"

"But, Lord, what about the time I broke all Ten Commandments in ten minutes!"

"Wow, that's heavy stuff. But I don't see any mention of it. Come in. The celebration's starting!"

"But, Lord," you say, trying one last time, "what about the times I hurt Kathie?"

"Now Yancy, that's very serious because she's one of my children, but there's nothing in the Book of Life about it. Look, I'll let you see for yourself!"

So you look at a dazzling white page with your name inscribed on it and at the bottom you read: PAID IN FULL BY JESUS CHRIST.

8

Body Ministry

Charm can be deceptive and beauty doesn't last, but a woman who fears and reverences God shall be greatly praised.

Proverbs 31:30

Looking at Michie makes me sick. Sometimes I can hardly believe that we come from the same two parents. Michie has one of those model-slim figures that stops cars and causes accidents. And I'm one of the accidents! You know, kind of like a before and after ad—before! I try to console myself with the fact that I am not fat, but I'm not as skinny as I would like to be, either. I have dieted and exercised until it would have killed a weaker person, but it's all to no avail. I was so self-concious that I didn't even wear slacks my whole senior year in high school! And when I did a layout for *Ingenue* magazine I begged the photographer to shoot me only from the waist up. He just looked at me like I was crazy.

Before you get this image of me rolling around like hippopotamus, let me assure you that I am not in the least an obese person. I am simply a victim of what I call the skinny syndrome. The majority of the women in this country will never grace the pages of America's fashion magazines, not because we are overweight, but because we aren't emaciated! Most of us are not 5'9" tall, and most of us don't weigh 105 pounds. But over the years the advertising agencies have convinced us that, regardless of varying bone structure, heredity, or metabolism, we should all wear a size seven and look great in slacks. How many girls do you know who fit this description? I'll bet that if they don't, they sure are miserable trying to attain it.

I mention this because I'm concerned that so many girls are discouraged in life because they are not the image they see in the fashion magazines. Madison Avenue has brainwashed our society as to what *beautiful* is; and if you're not skinny or don't wear your hair in a certain way or use just a certain shade of rouge on your cheeks, you aren't beautiful! That kind of philosophy has got to be one of the most blasphemous mockeries of God's handiwork!

In Psalms 139 we read: "You made all the delicate, inner parts of my body, and knit them together in my mother's womb. Thank you for making me so wonderfully complex! It is amazing to think about. Your workmanship is marvelous—and how well I know it!" (verses 13, 14). How well do *you* know it? Do you still look at other girls who are prettier than you and ask God why He made a mistake with you? Or do you accept your appearance, but secretly envy another girl's talent? Why is it that we are never satisfied with what we have? Do we dare insult God by thinking that it just isn't enough?

There will always be those individuals who are less attractive or more attractive on the outside than we are. There is just so much you can do to improve the way you look! But the potential for *inward beauty* is absolutely unlimited! It simply depends on how much you're willing to let Jesus cleanse and beautify you.

In my travels I have come across hundreds of women who were not the least bit threatened by my appearance or singing ability. They knew who they were and where they fit in the Body of Christ. That is the secret of true peace, for we cannot love others as Christ commands until we can first love ourselves. And that means loving ourselves as Jesus does—every pimple, every kinky hair, and every extra pound! Otherwise it is impossible to really love those pimple-less, smooth-haired "sticks" we admire so much.

God has not made a mistake with you. Believe it or not, you are *exactly* the way He planned you to be! Does it still seem unfair? I have this theory that I call the *theory of limitless limitation*. The first part is easy: God has given you special abilities to be used for His unique purpose. Now here is where I may lose a few of you: God has also given you special "inabilities" to be used for His unique purpose. These inabilities are just as much a part of His plan for you! Sure, you can do great things through your own capabilities, but who gets the glory? *You* do. The real blessing comes from achieving great things through your limitations. Then there is no doubt but that God is glorified.

The Apostle Paul wrote, "When I am weak, then am I strong!" (*See* 2 Corinthians 12:10.) Paul was no different from you and me. As a human being he was probably just as frightened, just as frustrated, and just as incapable of fulfilling God's commands as we are. I'm sure he knew some lonely moments and some disheartening situations. But, as a Spirit-filled human being he allowed Christ to be strong *through* his weaknesses, for he went on to say, ". . . the less I have, the more I depend on him."

I have heard it said that the extent to which God will use us depends on how willing we are to "die." *Dying to self* is a daily struggle—it's a battle of will. And very few of us ever give up without a fight.

Beauty is definitely in the eye of the beholder. I happen to think that freckles are a most pleasing adornment— naturally, I'm freckle-less! However, I know girls who will not leave their house until they have painted over their freckles with a dark makeup. You just can't please everybody and you'll go crazy if you try. You have to face yourself in the morning each and every day; and you better like what you see, or your afternoon and evening are doomed already.

I don't mean that you shouldn't try to improve yourself, especially in an area such as your weight which so seriously affects your overall health. Or perhaps you have a skin problem that, out of embarrassment, keeps you from going out and getting involved. These are both areas that can be medically treated and will result in a lovelier you. Yes, by all means do everything in your power that will make you happy about yourself. Knowing you look nice helps you to feel nice inside, and there's nothing wrong with that! But don't lose sleep over things you cannot change. You'll only wake up in the morning with bags under your eyes, and nothing to show for it. I know that I make myself and those around me miserable when I constantly complain about a problem that has no solution. Michie gets so angry with me when I whine about my weight. That poor girl has put up with my diets and my midnight exercising for so long that she deserves a medal for endurance beyond the call of duty; and yet she suffers from the same disease, only in another form—she's obsessed with her teeth. Michie happens to have a set that she thinks are larger than desirable. Everybody else thinks they are unique and really add to her appearance, but she is convinced otherwise.

No one can assure you that you are beautiful. That confidence can only come from within the private person called you. It starts with believing without a doubt that God loves you and accepts you completely, exactly the way you are. Jesus did not die for perfect people. He died on the cross for sinners such as you and me for He said, ". . . It is the sick who need a doctor, not those in good health" (Luke 5:31).

Each one of us faces different battles every day, and our problems are as unique as we ourselves are. But the answer to all these problems is ironically the same: Jesus. He is as different to each one of us as we are to Him. Did you know that He calls us all by name? (*See* John 10:3.) That should make you feel special, because *you are special* to *Him!*

A very sad commentary on the advantages of being a Christian is that so many believers have negative, pessimistic outlooks on life. It actually affects their appearance! Have you ever met a Christian who proceeded to tell you about her love for the Lord in such a deadpan, unemotional way that she left you completely cold? Where is all the joy that we are supposed to have in abundance? I think that joy is the by-product of obedience to God's will for you. It's a soul celebration that comes from knowing you're a child of God. Joy results from a life built on three priorities: *J* for Jesus, first in your heart; *O* for others, right behind Him; and *Y* for yourself, always last. I like to say I do not dwell in *me*, but in *we*. Truly you find yourself by first losing yourself. Peter advised Christians, "Don't be concerned about the outward beauty that depends on jewelry, or beautiful clothes, or hair arrangement. Be beautiful inside, in your hearts, with the lasting charm of a gentle and quiet spirit which is so precious to God. That kind of deep beauty was seen in the saintly women of old, who trusted God . . ." (1 Peter 3:3–5).

I heard one of the finest messages on the Parable of the Talents while on a visit to Dallas, Texas. I had been thinking a great deal about how to use my ability to its fullest potential and had not yet arrived at a satisfactory conclusion. When the pastor began to speak I thought, *Darn, another sermon I've heard a million times before!* But as he started reading the Scriptures from Matthew 25:14–30,

I sensed that this time it was going to be told with a different perspective. If there's anything I appreciate, it's a new perspective on an old subject.

I had always wondered why Jesus even included a mention of the middle man—the one who was given two talents. After all, isn't the message the same if only the good man and the wicked man are described? The pastor pointed out that each man was entrusted with an amount of money in direct proportion to his abilities. That much I already knew. I also understood that the master was fully aware of each man's character and how much responsibility he could safely be given. What I had not noticed was that when the master returned to account for the money, he praised the first and second servants in exactly the same way! He was no more pleased with the first man's earnings than the second man's, even though the monetary difference was considerable. What impressed the master was that both men had been faithful with what they had originally been given.

You and I were not created equal. But we shall both be called to give an account, just like the three servants, of how we have spent our time and talents. We shall not be judged in relation to each other, but in proportion to what He entrusted to us when He first gave us life.

Luke is very direct: "Much is required from those to whom much is given, for their responsibility is greater" (*see* Luke 12:48). A gift is not a gift until it is given away. All the talent in the world is worth nothing until it serves a useful purpose. The most frustrated people I know are Christians who have not yet discovered how to use their abilities in the Body of Christ. They are like fingers trying to be feet, or eyes trying to be ears. It just doesn't work and it never will. In writing to the Christians at Corinth Paul says, "Now here is what I am trying to say: All of you together are the one body of Christ and each of you is a separate and necessary part of it" (1 Corinthians 12:27).

So the first step is to take your eyes off what the other girl is doing. She is trying to work out her own salvation with fear and trembling and doesn't need any help from you! In time the Holy Spirit will reveal to both of you His particular road for you to take. Your ministries will probably take you down different paths, like a fork in the road that eventually leads to the same place. No one can go with you or hold your hand—because Jesus is already holding it!

Sure, you've got hang-ups. We all do. But they exist for the same reason that we do: to glorify our Creator. Quit crying over the fact that you have no new shoes; you are bound to meet a person who has no shoes at all. Decide right now that you're not going to spend one more minute in frustration over your "problem," whatever it is. Instead, ask the Lord to help you overcome it and knock it off your list of importance. Even try to thank Him for it, knowing it is as much in His purpose for you as anything else. When you know where you are going and Who is taking you there, you will be at peace in a world designed by God exclusively for you. Nurture all of the good qualities in your character; start a beauty campaign in your mind! You *are* what you think about!

. . . Fix your thoughts on what is true and good and right. Think about things that are pure and lovely, and dwell on the fine, good things in others. Think about all you can praise God for and be glad about.

Philippians 4:8

For as he thinketh in his heart, so is he. . . .

Proverbs 23:7 KJV

9

Disc-Courage!

*Help me to prefer obedience to making money! Turn me
away from wanting any other plan than yours. Revive
my heart toward you. Reassure me that your promises are
for me, for I trust and revere you.*

Psalms 119:36–38

Michie and I have been singing together for seventeen
years. We have never known anything different. As tiny
children we would hold imaginary microphones (or ba-
nanas or hairbrushes or candles—anything!) in front of our
mouths and pretend we were performing before an ador-
ing audience of millions. My father began tape-recording
us almost before we could talk—but, oh, could we sing!
Even our brother, David, piped in occasionally, and together "The Three Little Epsteins" were captured live
for all posterity. To this day we still get the greatest kick
from playing and replaying those hilarious old tapes.

"Where's *de moo-sic,* Daddy?" I would demand, quite
expecting a full orchestral accompaniment. I was always
crushed when told I must sing without music. The show

must go on and it always did. Mom and Dad were both great music lovers and they tried to instill in us from our earliest years a tremendous appreciation and respect for music of all forms. Michie and I knew every Broadway-hit score by heart—long before we had ever heard of Elvis Presley. Daddy had been a jazz saxophonist for years, and he made sure that we knew *swing* was not something you did while flying through the air on a rope! Benny Goodman, George Gershwin, and Tommy Dorsey were household names, to be mentioned with only the greatest reverence. I could do a perfect imitation of Ethel Merman, and Michie would mimic Jeannette MacDonald's operettas all over the house.

Music was the most precious treasure we owned outside of each other. We were rich with it. However, very soon it became evident that Michie would be the singer of the family. She could hit notes that went beyond the piano keys and threatened the glass in our windows. I resigned myself to being the actress of the family. On the outside I was Sarah Heartburn, but inside I concealed a passionate desire to sing. I secretly vowed that I would someday awe the world with my vocal brilliance. At that point all I had was a brilliant imagination!

One day I asked my mother to take me to Michie's voice teacher for an evaluation of my singing ability. *I* knew I could sing—what was wrong with everybody else? I'll never forget those painful moments in her studio, standing beside the piano singing a few pitiful scales. My range consisted of seven notes at the most! When I had finished, the teacher turned and looked up at me and said with more than small amusement, "Kathie, stick to harmony."

I cried all the way home, but by the time we reached our driveway I was more determined than ever. My wounded pride had turned to fierce resolve! I was going to sing no matter what *anyone* thought! For a long time everyone thought I was just plain crazy, I certainly must have seemed so. But my point is, it doesn't matter if people believe in you as long as you believe in yourself. All the encouragement from others is worthless without that spark of faith burning inside *you*. "For I can do all things through Christ who strengthens me!" (*See* Philippians 4:13.) If you truly believe that Scripture there is absolutely no limit to what you can achieve!

Within three months of my ego-crushing trip to the voice teacher's studio, I held the talent award from Bowie's Junior Miss Pageant. No one was more shocked than I. Sure, I thought I would be able to sing, but three months was more than even *I* dreamed possible! I have treasured the talent awards far more than the city and state titles put together, for they represent a dream come true.

If only we could accept the fact that the Lord wants all of our desires to become realities. He also wants us to work at it so that we will know how to properly appreciate the results when our dreams do come true.

Perhaps the most fulfilling of my many wonderful experiences at Oral Roberts University was my two-year membership in the World Action Singers. Each member is given a full scholarship (I love Jesus, Jesus loves me, what others pay for, I'll get *free!*) in return for participation in the television and public-appearance outreach of

Oral Roberts's ministry. The group is composed of six guys
and six girls and is a vital part of the total ministry of
O.R.U. World Action provided a wonderful opportunity
for my development as a performer as well as a person.
We made numerous trips to Hollywood, California, for
recording and TV taping sessions. I was in a constant state
of excitement mixed with gratitude to be involved with
so many marvelously talented people in such a professional setting. Imagine working side by side with Ralph
Carmichael in a recording session! As if that wasn't
enough, imagine being surrounded by the most capable
and innovative musicians alive today. This impressed me
far more than the stars we came in contact with during
our specials.

I especially loved the atmosphere of excellence that
permeated our every activity. I learned from Bill Cole,
our music producer, not to be satisfied with anything less
than my greatest performance; that way I initiate a constant challenge to do better the next time around, without
getting too discouraged about what I have accomplished.
I became all too aware of the fact that many Christians do
a halfhearted job when we, of all people, should have a
zeal for perfection unparalleled in any field today. Suddenly I wanted to prove to the world that my God is an
excellent God who rejoices in the fine accomplishments of
His people. I wanted to do something with my talent that
would touch people musically, yes—but spiritually as well.
Touching a person's soul is the catalyst for changing him.
I think most people want to change but don't know how
to go about it. Resolutions are made at the outset of each

new year in hopes that they might miraculously be kept. They seldom are. Instead, February comes along and the same old habits return; the individual is left more frustrated than ever at his inability to change through his own power. Therein lies the answer: ". . . Not by might, nor by power, but by my Spirit, says the Lord of Hosts—you will succeed because of my Spirit, though you are few and weak" (Zechariah 4:6). In other words, *Let go and let God!*

I had been at O.R.U. for over two years when the Lord spoke to me once more in the same manner as He had during the summer camp. Michie was a sophomore at O.R.U. and was living in a dormitory across campus from me. She had come down with a serious flu infection and I was on my way to visit her when, once again, I heard the Voice inside my head.

"Kathie, you're going to do an album," it said.

"I am, Lord?"

"Yes, and you're going to call it *Kathie and Michie: Friends.*"

"But, Lord," I argued, "we don't write any music, and I wouldn't even know where to begin!"

"I want you to draw on My Body," the Lord said. "Think of all the friends you have that I have given talent to in this area. Share this vision with them, and I will prepare their hearts for the music I want them to give you." Then He added, "I will do the rest."

By the time I reached the lobby of Michie's dorm our conversation was over, yet I remembered every word. I mean, it's not often that I receive such direct guidance! Excitedly I entered Michie's room and shared what the

Lord had revealed to me. Together we bowed and committed the project to God and His care. I had no sooner closed her door behind me when I saw it: a large circular piece of paper with one word on it—*friends*. I froze in my tracks and gaped at it for several moments before I picked it up and took it in to show to Michie. I have never seen her as speechless as she was when she read that one boldly written word. To us, it was a sign from heaven and we praised God for His wonderful direction in our lives.

Leaving Oral Roberts University was a difficult step of faith, for wherever we are actively accepted and appreciated we tend to become very secure. However, security is not always the most challenging state in which you can find yourself. I began to dry up as a Christian from the lack of personal involvement with those in need. It was too easy for me to rely on the fellowship at O.R.U. for growth rather than nurturing a vital relationship with Jesus. I was starting to deeply miss my ministry away from Tulsa, and this void began to seriously affect my fulfillment at O.R.U. I loved the World Action ministry, but after two years I began to feel that I could be a more effective witness if I were out of school. The television camera had become a dear friend, but it was a poor substitution for the warmth and dynamism I had experienced from ministering to a *live* audience. Television evangelism easily becomes mechanical if you're not careful. When you've been involved in TV for a long time it's easy to lose contact with the needy world behind the cameras. I wanted to leave O.R.U. and the World Action Singers before that could happen to me. Without something vital to offer that One Individual, I had nothing authentic to offer the masses.

I was in Hollywood during the middle of my last semester to record the music for our upcoming Christmas special. Ralph Carmichael was conducting the band all morning, so I waited to talk to him when we broke for lunch. I was completely terrified to talk to Ralph about my plans. He has always been a living legend to me, and the thought of sharing my little dreams with such a man seemed absolutely absurd!

This kind of evaluation proved to be more than inaccurate—it was downright insulting! I should have realized that Ralph was the kind of person who would be interested and would listen to my plans regardless of their insignificance to him. If my dreams were important enough to me to share with him, that was good enough for Ralph.

I approached him hesitantly—surprised at my own shyness. "Ralph," I began, "do you think you might have a moment while I'm here this week to talk with me?"

"Kathie," he said, grinning beneath his famous walrus-size mustache, "that would be delightful."

Several days later I met with Ralph and Bill Cole over lunch. We were in the midst of taping the special at NBC in Burbank, so we crossed the street to a little restaurant for the two-hour break and settled into a comfortable booth. Although I had worked with both men for two years, I realized that I only knew them within the context of a professional setting. Even so, I was instantly at home with these warm and sensitive Christians who have done so much to revolutionize the worldwide outreach of religious music. My shyness seemed to melt away under their sincere interest in me. Before I realized my boldness, I shared with them the prophetic incident I had experienced outside Michie's dorm. Both men listened in silence as I recounted the conversation with the Lord I had had just months before. Then Ralph slowly lifted his gaze to mine and began to question me for the better part of an hour. He shared the philosophy on which his publishing company, Lexicon, is built and went on to describe the necessary ingredients for a successful album. His record company, Light Records, follows a policy of interest in communication, primarily, and then talent.

"We're interested in Kathie, the person," he said. "Talent is easy to come by around here. But real people are harder to find."

His words were like a melody to me. Before we arose to return to the TV taping, it was decided that *Kathie and Michie: Friends* had found a home at Light Records.

I have learned to listen without argument to the Voice of the One who calls me by name. "You know very well that God's promises to you have all come true" (Joshua 23:14). I have always envied the fact that the Jehovah of the Old Testament spoke audibly to His people concerning His will for their lives. How much easier it would be for us if He continued in that practice today! And yet He does in so many wonderful ways. He instructs us through His Word, through circumstances, and through prayer. Sometimes He even speaks to us as in the days of old!

10

California or Bust

Don't let others spoil your faith and joy with their philosophies, their wrong and shallow answers built on men's thoughts and ideas, instead of on what Christ has said. For in Christ there is all of God in a human body; so you have everything when you have Christ. . . .

Colossians 2:8–10

Ever since I was a little girl I had dreamed of living in Hollywood. I suppose deep within each child's imagination there dwells the dream of some faraway place where the sun shines all the time and wishes all come true. Well, when I first came to my dreamland, California, it rained for five straight weeks!

I left Tulsa on March 19 and flew into Los Angeles International Airport, hoping to discover upon arrival God's plan for my life. Judy Baxter, a friend from my days at O.R.U., had moved to California after graduation and taken a job as a page at NBC in Burbank. She met my plane and we started on the half-hour drive to her apartment in Glendale, where I was to stay until I received some Divine direction.

There are times in each Christian's life when the only direction one has is seemingly none at all in the eyes of the world. This was the situation I faced at the time I made the decision to come to L.A. I had only an inner prodding that said, *Go and find out. You'll never know until you try.* I have found that one of the greatest sources of conflict in many of my friends' lives is *regret* over plans or dreams or hopes that never materialized—not because they were impossible to attain, but because they were undertaken halfheartedly or allowed to be swept aside by more "practical" matters. With the passing of time it is possible for these dreams, once the energetic spark of their imagination, to become a blazing fire which burns away at their daily contentment. We begin to resent the fact that we didn't go on that trip when we had the freedom, we didn't go to college when we had the chance, we didn't work on that project when we had the time. Whatever it is that we had failed to do may cause us to be dissatisfied with what we are presently doing.

As a musician, I used to look back with real disappointment on my parents' efforts to interest me in my piano lessons. I wanted to do anything but practice those scales; today I find my inability to play a musical instrument a very difficult obstacle to overcome in my career. So whom do I resent? My parents—because they weren't strict or clever enough to trick me into practicing? Or do I blame myself and mentally impose self-punishment each time I watch someone walk over and effortlessly begin to make music? Or do I just make excuses for myself? "I was only a child . . . how could I know that it would harm me later in life?"

Each of us has the power to choose any or all of the above reactions, but that is all that it amounts to—reactions. Reactions are not solutions. I'm learning that if I can't handle a situation in my mind without a conflict of some kind, that situation is one that has yet to be turned over to God. How many times have we battled with the same thought processes, only to wear ourselves out by the game of mental ping-pong. It is only when we face our problem squarely, call it by name, and seek the Lord's correction that we will see a permanent change in our behavior.

I am not an advocate of arbitrarily "doing your own thing," but I am a believer in deliberately seeking out those areas in my life that I feel are unfulfilled, discovering why they are there, and then asking the Lord to find their completion in Him. If there is a strong, immovable inclination within you, you can bet that there is just as strong a reason for it! So many times we feel that our desires in life should be ignored. Somewhere we latched onto the idea that this is the true Christian way of selfless sacrifice! In doing so, I think we often thwart God's plans for something He originally placed there for His glory. It is so easy to confuse God's will with what you think is your own evil self-will. In some cases it may very well be, but that is the very reason why you must explore every possibility! It is dangerous to harbor secret guilts over your secret desires: sometimes the guilt turns into resentment toward God and you think, *Lord, why can't I have that?* All the while God has been trying to say, "Well, I never said that you couldn't!" Perhaps any question within your own mind could be settled by just asking God. Does that sound too simple? The Bible says we *have* not because we *ask* not. (*See* James 4:2.) I believe the Lord would welcome any inquiry on your part as to His will for your life. If that stubborn yearning in your heart is not of Him, ask Him to show you that fact by causing it to diminish as He replaces it with a new direction—this time His Perfect one.

I don't understand the logic behind it, but for some reason being a professional entertainer is not accepted with great enthusiasm or encouragement from the Christian community. "What does a nice Christian girl like you want to do *that* for?" became the favorite question of many "concerned" fellow believers. I heard this so many times from so many people that I began to wonder, myself, if the desire to perform had been placed within me by the devil after all. *It must be wrong,* I thought, *I feel too good when I'm doing it!*

In this way Satan used many unsuspecting, well-intentioned Christians to hinder God's perfect plan for me. It was a long time and a hard struggle before I finally came to realize the wonderful, liberating truth that God really loves me; He has an exciting plan for my life, and He has placed certain skills, dreams, feelings, and desires within me just to accomplish that very plan. With guilt gone, I now have new eyes to see myself and a new ability to allow Him to channel everything as He sees fit.

In his book *Power in Praise* Merlin R. Carothers says, "God has a very special plan for your life. . . . He formed you lovingly, carefully, exactly to His specifications, every detail just as He wanted it—your looks, your abilities, your place of birth, the family. . . . Nothing about you or your life has been accidental up to this point. In love He reached out and drew you to Himself through circumstances He had arranged just for that purpose. . . . And now God's plan is to make you full and complete!" But how do we become full and complete?

Each of us faces unique problems on our individual roads to perfection. We have all achieved in some areas and failed in others. Most of us have known love in some form or another, but some of us have never felt a loving touch or heard a loving word. There are those among us who are scarred emotionally; some are scarred physically, for the rest of their days. And some of us have known Christ since we were young, while others are meeting Him for the first time today. Yes, our pasts are varied, but our promise for the future is exactly the same: "For because of our faith, he has brought us into this place of highest privilege where we now stand, and we confidently and joyfully look forward to actually becoming all that God has had in mind for us to be" (Romans 5:2).

Now, it's obvious to everyone who knows me that I am not yet all that Christ designed me to be—far from it! But this is hardly defeat! I can rejoice, for I know that each day brings me closer to Jesus, and therefore closer to His level of holiness! I don't have to carry the burden of self-perfection for I know, without a doubt, that Jesus has already worked out the blueprints and already begun the construction that will result in the final product. Sometimes I feel like crying out, "Please be patient—God is not finished with me yet!" But even so, I press toward the goal of the high calling of Jesus Christ (*see* Philippians 3:14). Isn't it thrilling to think that someday we shall reach our goal?

I'm more amazed every day as I sit back and watch God construct even the smallest detail of my life. He is a master architect and I can almost feel the solid rock beneath my feet, the strong walls of protection around me, and the comforting ceiling of His everlasting love. There are still many rooms within my personality that need to beautified before I become the mansion He designed me to be, but I have a lifetime ahead of me to let Him decorate the interior! I no longer worry about my inability to play the piano. Somehow I know God is big enough to work through my inadequacies. As soon as you realize that He can turn any disadvantage into an advantage you have come into a greater awareness of His power in your life.

When I was fourteen, I began singing with Michie in a folk group called "Pennsylvania Next Right." Together with five boys from our community, we began performing in coffeehouses, churches, school assemblies—wherever they were desperate enough to have us! My parents were excited that we had finally found a healthy outlet for our frustrated musical talents. However, others were far from enthusiastic! It didn't take long for the news to spread that Kathie and Michie were singing songs about revolution and drugs and sex with a bunch of hippies! Unfortunately, this had the effect of setting us against believing that the church could be a vehicle for presenting our witness in music. It just didn't seem a very conducive atmosphere for developing or expanding one's talent! I'm glad to see that this is changing, and churches are beginning to accept their responsibility to provide freedom of expression within the Body. What a difference it would have made in my life many years ago! Instead, we traveled and ministered in our own way wherever we could. We sang in army hospitals for the battered veterans of the war in Vietnam and came away with a new appreciation for our healthy, whole bodies. We probably did appear in some places that were considered less than spiritual in atmosphere, but not once did we leave without sharing in some way the Light of our lives. And at times it was hard to do because none of the other members of the group shared our commitment to Christ; in fact, most were downright embarrassed! But if they wanted Michie and me, they had to take Jesus too. He was part of the team.

The memory of those days passed quickly before me now, as we neared Judy's apartment. Would I be able to take Jesus along now, too? Would I have the strength to share Christ in Hollywood with some of the most "liberated," successful, and experienced people in the field? Suddenly I felt very small indeed and I marveled that the Lord should think me capable of such a witness. But I knew one thing for sure: the grace of God was *still* leading me, and that meant that He was *still* keeping me. Sometimes that is the only comfort we know, but it's definitely all we need.

I literally spent the first two weeks in California on my feet and on the telephone. I visited every person I knew and called every person I didn't. If my pride weighed anything at all, I'm sure I would have lost twenty pounds from the beating it took during those first traumatic weeks. "Why are you here?" "What are you going to do?" "What do you have going for you?" These were questions I faced at every turn. For each question I could only truthfully answer, "I don't know."

I came to California because I knew I had to, it's as simple as that. Oral Roberts had a phrase he used whenever he was asked how he was sure of God's will. He would say, "I know that I know that I know that I know." Now *I* know what he means! Even though I had never felt so insecure or so frightened, I still had that crazy inner peace that only other Christians can comprehend. To every person I spoke with I must have seemed like the thousands of other young girls who leave their small-town homes and travel to the big city in search of their future. I knew the difference, though—He makes all the difference in the world!

11

Show Girl—Show Jesus

*But my God shall supply all your need according to his
riches in glory by Christ Jesus.*

Philippians 4:19 KJV

I have discovered that God can take me through any
circumstance as long as I trust Him to care for me along
the way. He often uses His children to accomplish just
that. Judy's kindness when I first arrived in California
helped me to overcome the loneliness and the strange-
ness of being in a new environment. But when her roommate was due to return, I had to ask the Lord to find me
a new place to stay. If He wanted me to remain in Los
Angeles, He was going to have to provide a place *without
my asking!* I am not the kind of person who can easily ask
for favors. I don't know if I'm too proud or too inhibited!
I have a distinct feeling that I'm too proud, but I don't like
to admit it!

One night I began to pray about the problem before
me: "Lord, I really believe You led me to California.
Okay, here I am, so now what? Father, I have so many

needs. I wish I could just come to You in thanksgiving without asking for a thing, but I can't right now. Lord, I'm lonely and hurt and I feel so rejected. Nobody seems to care about me as a person or as a performer—good grief, Lord, I don't even have a place to stay!"

My list of requests seemed endless as I continued to pray. I was just convinced that I needed *instant answers.* I have since come to realize that God is in the business of meeting needs, but in His time and in His way. If we don't have something right now it's because we don't actually need it! We'll know for sure when we do need it because that is when He will give it to us!

The Bible says, "Your heavenly Father already knows perfectly well what you need and He will give it to you if you give Him first place in your life and live as He wants you to. So don't be anxious about tomorrow. God will take care of your tomorrow too. Live one day at a time" (*see* Matthew 6:32–34).

I learned the truth of this Scripture as I watched God begin to work things out one by one as I trusted Him day by day.

I have been close friends with Tim Archer since my first year at O.R.U. Tim is the leader of one of the finest Christian rock groups in the country—The Archers. I admire these musicians enormously for their obvious talent, but I love them dearly for their dedication to a life on the road, sharing Jesus. I've often wondered if I could handle such a devoted life-style. I'm sure glad they do!

Easter morning dawned incredibly bright as Tim and Judy and I attended services at the Hollywood Bowl. How good it was of the Lord to bring the sunshine on the most glorious day of all, after so many days of rain! From our seats we could look beyond the stage, across the mountains, and see perfectly, in the distance, a large empty cross outlined against the morning sky. I couldn't help thinking that the first Easter must have been just as perfect.

During lunch afterwards, Tim asked me the inevitable question of what I planned to do now.

"I'm not really sure," I answered, "the Lord is going to have to work out a lot of things. For one, Judy's roommate gets back next week so I have to find a new place to stay."

"Well," he said casually, "you could stay at my apartment."

"Tim Archer!" I cried. "What would the saints think?"

Tim just laughed and answered, "Kathie, that wasn't a proposition! We're going on tour for seven weeks and the apartment will be empty, so you might as well watch over it for us. Besides," he added, "it'll be nice to come home to a clean house!"

I moved into The Archers' apartment and wondered what God was up to next. The answer came a few weeks later while I was visiting Dick Ross at his office. Dick had been the producer of the "Oral Roberts Presents" shows when I was a World Action Singer and he had always impressed me as a sensitive and warm individual. I told him that I was looking for someone who could handle my secular activities—TV, commercials, and such. However, I wanted a person I could trust, and one who really understood what I was and was not willing to do as a Christian in show business. Dick offered to call Dorothy Day Otis and set up an appointment for me to meet her.

I had heard of Dorothy through many people; one of these was Tink Wilkerson, who called me before our interview to wish me well. Tink is a very successful car salesman in the Midwest and one of the finest Christian laymen I have ever been privileged to know. "Uncle Tink" and his wife, Sue, became my folks away from home while I was at O.R.U. where Tink is a regent. I had no idea at the time just how much God intended to use them in my life away from Tulsa. Tink is probably one of Kathryn Kuhlman's closest friends and advisors. He often leaves his business in Oklahoma to travel with her throughout the country, and it is a great deal because of him that I came to be the female soloist on Miss Kuhlman's Sunday-morning television programs.

Dorothy and I hit it off from the very beginning. I liked her kind yet confident manner. She really made me feel comfortable as I sat across from her and shared my plans and hopes for the future. I could tell she was anxious to share something, and very soon I discovered the reason behind her excitement.

Four and a half years earlier, Dorothy and her husband, Don, were both expected to die within a short period of time. Don was suffering from acute emphysema and Dorothy could hardly walk due to a double curvature of her spine. Sitting there by her desk I could hardly believe it —the woman in front of me was obviously a very healthy, attractive, and active person! What had happened?

"We had heard about Kathryn Kuhlman, so we decided

to go to her meeting at the Shrine Auditorium as a final resort. We went, and nothing happened to us. Other people experienced divine healings, but Don and I left exactly as we came." Dorothy grew more excited now; it was evident she loved sharing what happened next.

"For some reason, we went back to the Shrine the next month. We just couldn't forget the experience of being at one of Miss Kuhlman's meetings. This time both of us could feel the Holy Spirit going through our bodies! It was so marvelous," Dorothy beamed, "and we've never been the same since!"

Then Dorothy carefully brought out and showed me the worn and fading X rays that have become her greatest treasure.

"Isn't it silly that these dirty old things have become so precious?" She layed them down, then smiled at me and said, "You know, Don and I accepted Christ that same day we were healed, and that's the *greatest miracle of all!*"

Our Heavenly Father must have the most terrific sense of humor. How ironic that I should find myself sitting in a major Hollywood agency and rejoicing with one of the industry's top agents over God's miraculous love!

Careers progress slowly for most performers in show business. Only a very few enjoy instant success. It didn't take very long for me to realize how long it takes!

I was used to seeing immediate results from my efforts, so the months of waiting for pictures, composites, interviews, and "breaks" were difficult ones. I just can't imagine how people without Christ make it though the rough times without losing their minds. It takes an incredible amount of confidence to even go through an audition or an interview for a job; when you are rejected time after time, your self-image begins to suffer enormously. If I hadn't truly believed that Jesus loved me, I think I would have become so permanently discouraged that I would have left and gone home long before my "big break" was due to arrive. Hollywood has its glamour, yes. But, for the most part, show business is full of insecurity, disappointment, and (when you're lucky enough to get it) very hard work!

Very soon after I had signed a year's contract with her agency, Dorothy called me with the news that I was scheduled to audition for Kathryn Kuhlman the following day at CBS, where she was in the midst of taping her television show.

"Just to be safe," Dorothy concluded, "be sure to bring some long dresses in case she wants to use you on a show."

I got up at six the next morning to begin vocalizing. Hurriedly I downed some hot tea, grabbed a bunch of clothes from the closet and raced to the studio—only to be told I was at the wrong CBS! How was I supposed to know there are three CBS locations?

With only minutes left before my appointment, I battled the rush-hour traffic to downtown Hollywood and stumbled onto the set with only moments to spare. I was hardly in a relaxed attitude when Dorothy took me over to meet Kathryn Kuhlman! She looked at me as only Kathryn Kuhlman can and led me to the piano where she deposited me with a laughing command, "Okay, sing!"

I can't remember what I sang or how it sounded, but

instantly that ageless face was in front of me whispering repeatedly, "It's adorable." The next thing I knew I was singing "Amazing Grace" before four television cameras! I had gotten dressed, had my makeup done, and my hair rolled and styled—all in ten minutes! When God wants something to happen, *it happens!*

Driving back to Tim's apartment I marveled again at God's wonderful way of working out even the smallest details of our lives. I could hardly wait to share the news with everybody at the Bible study that night.

Fellowship with other believers is important to every Christian's growth; but at this point in my life, I found it to be absolutely essential to my *remaining* a Christian, much less growing as one! So I started attending a study I had heard of that is led by Paul Johnson. Paul, a successful Christian composer and arranger, had begun the study in his home to disciple the increasing numbers of new show-business believers. Many studio singers had come to know Christ through working with Paul in recording sessions, and now he sensed a real responsibility to lead them into a deeper dimension of understanding. What a blessing it became for me! I would go in depressed and dried up and come away joyful and overflowing once again. Here were brothers and sisters who shared the same difficulties in their walk with Christ because we all lived in the same world, were involved in the same type of work, and therefore faced the same problems every day. Paul's Bible-study group met a need in me that had never before been met. I realized then that God had a permanent place for me in California.

As permanent as it was meant to be, it wasn't long before I was off again—this time to a place I never dreamed possible!

"How would you like to go to Las Vegas?" Paul called me one day.

"What?" I cried. "You've got to be kidding!"

But he was serious. It seems that one of the singers in a trio had dropped out of a show that was scheduled to open that very next night, and the producer was desperately looking for a replacement. Paul convinced me that it was a family-type show, so four hours later my plane landed in Las Vegas, and I was whisked off to rehearsal. To this day I do not know how the Lord handled it, but the next night we opened in "Country Music, USA" at the Landmark Hotel. Any one of the World Action Singers can tell you that I am not famous for my sight-reading ability, yet somehow I learned that music as quickly as if I had known it all my life. I believe with all my heart that God gives us what we need, when we need it. What a comforting thought!

I didn't struggle for one moment with guilt over performing in Las Vegas; in fact, the very opposite is true— I *knew* I was to be there! The Lord gave me countless opportunities to share His light in one of the darkest cities in the world! I have been asked many times how I managed to maintain a strong witness in a place so obviously unchristian. People are surprised when I tell them it was one of the easiest ministries I have ever undertaken. I was so completely "out of place" in Las Vegas that I couldn't help shining out like a giant neon sign! As a

Christian, I am always struggling with the gray areas of sin in my life—those things not specifically spelled out in the Bible, but left up to the believer's sensitivity as to what's right and what's wrong, depending on where and with whom! But in Las Vegas sin is so blatant—it's so *obvious* —that it's easy to avoid! I stayed at the Landmark, doing two shows a night for twenty-eight straight days, and it was a tremendous experience. At no time was there a question in my mind as to how to conduct myself, what to share, or what to show—*Jesus,* of course!

12

The Quiet Riot

*But whenever anyone turns to the Lord from his sins,
then the veil is taken away. The Lord is the Spirit who
gives them life, and where he is there is freedom.... But
we Christians have no veil over our faces; we can be
mirrors that brightly reflect the glory of the Lord. And
as the Spirit of the Lord works within us, we become
more and more like him.*

2 Corinthians 3:16–18

How many times have you heard: "Why can't you let
your hair down and just be real?" or "She just doesn't
seem real."? Lately it seems that the word *real* has been
cropping up constantly in my life, and I can't help but
wonder how much significance it has to my relationship
with Christ and with others.

Obviously we live in a very real world—a physical
world full of real people, real places, and very real experiences that have a profound effect upon our everyday
lives. A wave of realism expressed in movies, books,
philosophies, and politics is sweeping across our country.

Americans were recently shocked by the reality of inconsistencies found at the highest levels in our government. To compensate for the lack of public trust politicians are campaigning under new claims of honesty and integrity, promising to face "the real issues" so vital to our future and the future of the world. Real problems can be very frightening.

As Christians, we look forward with hope in our hearts to the new world coming when Christ sets up His Eternal Kingdom. But what do we do in the meantime while we are confined to physical bodies in a present, imperfect world of pain and problems? One criticism I have often heard regarding Christians is that they are "so spiritually minded, they're no earthly good." I think we do well to examine our personal attitude to discover if perhaps we, too, have been guilty of longing for that pie in the sky at the expense of the bread of life.

The Bible teaches that human beings were placed on this earth with the express purpose to glorify God the Creator. "For you are bought with a price, therefore glorify God in your body and in your spirit, which are God's" (*see* 1 Corinthians 6:20 KJV). I don't think it is possible to glorify God at all without cultivating the quality of being real.

Being real necessitates being honest. Take a good look at yourself—what do you see? Are you one of those individuals who is afraid of failing, afraid of losing, or (most painful thought of all) being rejected? If you are like many Christians, you probably find yourself "keeping face" while harboring internally a great many inconsistencies.

What "seems" is very rarely what "is."

I was not aware until recently that I, too, was guilty of just such falseness. For many years I wondered why I was always misunderstood. I couldn't understand why people struggled when they first met me to accept that I really was as I appeared. Inevitably they would come to realize that I naturally *was* happy, I *was* affectionate, and I *was* outgoing—but it took them so long to believe it!

"What am I doing wrong, Lord?" I would ask Him. "Obviously I am guilty of something that is causing these people to react this way at first."

Eventually the Lord revealed to me that I was confusing His desire for me to be a blessing to others with my pride at being so! It got to the point where I would not leave my room at O.R.U. until I felt that I could smile and minister to others, rather than burden them with my own problems. As a result, I appeared to be an ever-happy, carefree, and contented Christian, and nothing could be further from the truth! Yes, I have a constant peace and an untouchable joy, but I also have moments of depression, frustration, and doubt just like everybody else! The fact is, I was too proud to admit it! I rationalized that my hesitation to share problems was my concern not to burden others, when the truth is I didn't want anyone to think I *had* problems!

It literally revolutionized my life to realize I don't have to be a spiritual giant in everyone's eyes to be a sincere Christian. No one expects me to be a bulwark for all seasons! Once I realized this, I entered a whole new degree of intimacy in my relationships with Christian friends. For the first time they could relate to me as a fellow human being! I no longer needed to mask my problems—now I could share them!

I must bestow most of the credit for this enlightenment in my life on Tom Netherton. Tom is a very popular regular on TV on the "Lawrence Welk Show," a client with Fishers of Men Opportunities, Inc., and a beautiful brother in the Lord. One evening we were discussing the difficulty of being real—especially in a notoriously phoney place like Hollywood! Both Tom and I, and most of our show-business friends, sense a definite responsibility to share Christ in our professional relationships. Strangely enough, we find it a great deal easier to be real on the job than to be honest with each other! All we have to do is look around us, in a studio or on a set, to realize how lucky we are to know Jesus Christ! Our natural inclination is to describe the happiness in Him to those without Him! But the minute we are confronted with the private opportunity to share with each other, we close up and retreat behind the comfortable cliches that we all know so well.

"Tom, why is it that we're so afraid to be really honest with each other?" I asked him. "We of all people should have the freedom to be real because we're so secure in His love for us."

"I know, Kathie. But we don't want people to think we're unhappy in any way because that must mean we're not *spiritual*—not letting Christ control our lives. I guess we just don't want them to think that we've failed."

"But we all have, Tom!" I said. "And we all know that everyone does. Why the hang-up with letting others help us through the times when we need them most?"

Tom thought about it a minute, then answered, "I guess it all comes down to being vulnerable. We don't want to take the risk of having someone see us as we really are because there's always the chance they won't like what they see." The impact of his statement must have hit him then because he grew pensive and added, "It's more secure to stay behind the walls we build around us to protect ourselves. We don't experience the intimacy that comes from being vulnerable—but at least we're safe!"

The more we discussed this, the more I realized how pervasive the problem was in me. I was a "real" phoney! I finally saw the need to relax and be myself—even if the real me was a real failure! Only then could Jesus be the real Victory.

Many times since that evening with Tom, I have been tempted to sail back once again into the protective harbor of phoniness. Each time something inside me says, *Don't do it, Kathie! Take a chance on being rejected. Risk it and experience the freedom of being real!*

The Apostle Paul knew how attractive the world could be and how easily a Christian could be tempted to conform, simply out of the need to belong somewhere. He warns us, "Don't let the world around you squeeze you into its own mold, but let God remold your minds from within, so that you may prove in practice that the plan of God for you is good, meets all his demands and moves toward the goal of true maturity." (*See* Romans 12:2 PHILLIPS.)

Love always carries with it a high price. Freedom al-

ways carries with it a responsibility. California is known
for its progressive, permissive atmosphere. Deviation
from the norm is usually applauded as a victory for self-
expression. I do not agree with the concept of *personal
freedom* as it applied to the "revolution generation" because it's far too dangerous! Such a concept implies "do
your own thing" without the responsibility of its effects,
and this results in anarchy. I think, however, this idea can
have a great deal of validity for Christians who realize that
true freedom comes from joyfully facing our responsibilities to God, ourselves, and each other. Jesus did say, "You
will know the truth and the truth will set you free" (*see*
John 8:32). When we know Jesus—Truth, Himself—we
become liberated to do our own thing in Him! This is the
quiet riot. When we fall in love with God, everything else
falls into place in our lives; we have priorities, we have
direction. And through asking Him for it, we can have
wisdom to deal with the freedom He gives us.

We have a tremendous responsibility to accept the
workings of the Holy Spirit within each other. If you don't
like something another Christian is involved in, your best
course of action is to pray for that person. God always
separates the sin from the sinner. He hates the sin, but He
loves the sinner. Should we do less? Speaking the truth in
a spirit of love is an art that few of us have mastered. Most
of the time we respond to spiritual matters on a purely
human level. Our motives are usually commendable—we
just don't want to see that person get hurt or that situation
get out of hand. But our actions are rarely as commendable as our intentions. Human beings have a terrific way

of getting in God's way!

I'm so grateful that God shows us our weaknesses just to help us become stronger in Him. There is no condemnation, just gentle correction that builds us up as children of God. And I'm grateful that Jesus has presented Himself as a living example for us to follow on our way to being *real*.

13

Hallelujah for Love!

I will sing to the Lord because he has blessed me so richly.

Psalms 13:6

I've been having a love affair with an older man for years—but it's alright, he's my father. I guess I'm one of the lucky ones. I never ran away from him, I always ran right to him; we would talk it over, and soon I would feel much better. My father is a rare individual and quite a character in the eyes of the world.

His name is Aaron Leon Epstein, but he is affectionately known to all as "Eppie." His father was a full-blooded Russian Jew and Daddy was blessed to inherit the famous Jewish business sense. I couldn't have been more than five years old when Daddy first started instilling this kind of wisdom in me! My brother and sister and I worked all week doing household chores for which we received a skimpy allowance on Saturday morning. To compensate for this meager amount, we established a thriving corner store when I was six; by the time I was eight years old, I

was editor-in-chief of the *Children's Post,* a weekly neighborhood newspaper. You might say even if we weren't the
richest kids in town, we sure were the most enterprising!

Even as a small child I learned not only the value of the
dollar, but also the greater value of pride in my accomplishments. It saddens me to think that so many children
never experience this inner pride or the self-confidence
which grows from it because they never have to work.
Their parents give them everything they want because
it's easier than supervising their activities while they earn
it. As a result, the children are cheated of one of life's
greatest satisfactions. It can, and often does, cripple them
for the rest of their lives. Children who are given everything they want grow into adults who naturally expect the
same treatment. Life is a shock when they are forced to
make a living or go without food and a shelter over their
heads.

You can probably count on one hand the number of
people you know who really enjoy their work. If you're
like me, most of the people you know spend one-third of
their entire day in a business situation they detest. You
know this has to have an adverse effect on the other two-
thirds of their time! Unhappiness at work creates frustration and, ultimately, unhappiness at home.

Certainly this is sad for the unbeliever; but it is so much
sadder for the Christian who does not have to suffer
through, but so often does. We live beneath our privileges
as children of God! And this insults the God who has so
much more to offer!

Jesus said, "The thief's purpose is to steal, kill and destroy. My purpose is to give life in all its fullness" (John 10:10). This fullness includes the office, too! In the kitchen, or behind the counter, or on the stage, or in the tractor, or behind the pulpit, or wherever we earn a living is where God wants to be—with us in all His fullness. He loves the department-store clerk as much as the African missionary, for both are ministers in the truest sense of the word. Your mission field as a Christian is where you live, work, and play, and your responsibility is to share the hope that is within you with the people you confront in your daily surroundings. You can do as much for the Lord in your office, by the way you smile and love others, as your sister in South America can do when she ministers with medicine and food. It all depends on your attitude.

Perhaps the most important thing I have learned in my twenty-two years is the natural law that after every valley there follows a mountaintop. You cannot reach that mountain, though, until you have first traveled through the valley and emerged victorious. Praise for the valley experience becomes like the wings of a bird that soars you upward to the very peak of the mountain that once seemed so faraway.

My father has always told me, "Kathie, I love you too much to deny you the privilege of making mistakes." This is a perfect picture of our Heavenly Father's love for us, too; for each time we can rise after a fall, we are stronger and wiser than before we stumbled. No matter what valley we are suffering through right now, there is a message of hope for us:

Oh, sing to him you saints of his; give thanks to his holy
name. His anger lasts a moment; his favor lasts for life!
Weeping may go on all night, but in the morning there
is joy.

                                                    Psalms 30:4, 5

Even at the moments of greatest crisis when it was
absolutely impossible for my father to be angrier at me,
I knew in my heart that it was only a matter of time before
I would snuggle into forgiving arms and hear him tell me
once again how much he loved me. He would wipe the
tears from my eyes and somehow this would wipe the hurt
away too. The same scene would be repeated over and
over again, but each new act of forgiveness brought to me
a greater assurance of my father's love.

What a distorted picture so many of us have of our
Heavenly Father! We cannot fathom a young child rush-
ing excitedly to her father crying, "Daddy, Daddy, I love
you so much!" and her father replying to her, "Good, I've
been waiting for you a long time to tell me that you love
me. Now I'm going to take away all your toys and your
favorite teddy bear too!" It makes absolutely no sense. Yet
this concept of a cruel, demanding, grabbing God with
fire in His nostrils is an all too common one among Christians and non-Christians alike. We insult God Almighty
with our fears and our frustrations!

We need have no fear of someone who loves us perfectly;
his perfect love for us eliminates all dread of what he

might do to us. If we are afraid, it is for fear of what he might do to us, and shows that we are not fully convinced that he really loves us. So you see, our love for him comes as a result of his loving us first.

1 John 4:18

There is nothing more beautiful than the unconditional love of Christ. Unlike its human counterpart, Christ's love does not seek a return or a reward. It saddens me to think that much of our love for each other is predicated on *if.* So many Christians are hung up on denominationalism that they think Jesus would only visit their church were He to physically come to earth again! That's nonsense! I like the answer a friend of mine gave when asked what religion she practiced. She just smiled and said, "Well, I'm a Baptist strictly by *choice,* but I'm a Christian strictly by *grace!*" We only harm our witness for Christ by arguing amongst ourselves, for we cannot love and minister to the lost, if we the saved are in disharmony. Jesus said, "I demand that you love each other as much as I love you. And here is how to measure it—the greatest love is shown when a person lays down his life for his friends" (John 15:12, 13).

How we must grieve the Lord by our lack of love and concern for each other! Real love is not the tokenism displayed by a quick "Yeah, brother, I'm real sorry to hear about that. Look, I've gotta run, but I'll be prayin' for ya!" That isn't Christian compassion, it's a mockery of it! Yet some of us practice it religiously.

The pure love of Jesus has been ministered to me in so many ways, by so many people, that it would take another book itself to mention them all. Many think that Christianity would die from lack of practice if it were up to Christians. In many ways this is true, but there are always those rare individuals who actually live their faith and keep Christ alive and well on the Planet Earth.

Howard and Julie Twilley are two such people. Howard is one of the original Miami Dolphin football players, and his wife, Julie, is a teacher of Marabel Morgan's Total Woman course. I stayed at the Twilley home one summer while we were filming our "Oral Roberts Presents" Sunday-morning programs in Tulsa. I dreaded spending the long lonely months at the dormitory; so they insisted I stay at their home until we finished taping, and I went home for my summer vacation. Naturally I was thrilled at the invitation!

Julie is the epitome of the *Total Woman.* She does not teach one concept that she does not try to practice while at home. I know, I watched her for two months! During that time Julie never once asked me to repay their generosity in any way. I was expected to enjoy the privileges of the family members and the responsibilities of the family's guests! I was never asked to make my bed, clear the table, or change little Michael one time! Julie showered me with such pure love that I gained a new perspective on the nature of love itself. Because I was not expected to, I did far more than if I had been asked! I began to cherish Howard and Julie's love so much that I just naturally wanted to live up to the measure of love they had shown me!

Love can only grow in a loving, nurturing atmosphere. This is the way God loves us—not *because* of what we are, but *in spite* of it! Knowing that God loved me enough to send His Only Son to die for me creates in me a desire to reciprocate this love to God. He is One who *does* deserve it!

God asks us: "Be still, and know that I am God" (*see* Psalms 46:10 KJV). Sometimes I think this is the hardest thing in the world to do. Inactivity is just impossible for me! Yet now I have come to understand that by *being still* He means:

> Don't worry about anything; instead, pray about everything; tell God your needs and don't forget to thank him for his answers. If you do this you will experience God's peace, which is far more wonderful than the human mind can understand. His peace will keep your thoughts and your hearts quiet and at rest as you trust in Christ Jesus.
>
> Philippians 4:6, 7

I have come to truly believe that God is far less concerned with what we *do* for Him than with what we *are* for Him. It's a lot easier for Sarah Heartburn here to be a martyr and die for the cause, rather than get up every morning and smile and love Jesus all day long. Dying is far more dramatic and lots more glorious! Yet He wants me to live as a manifestation of His love while I am on this earth.

Jesus Christ was the only individual in history who was

ever born with the express purpose of dying. In dying He was the only One Being who ever accomplished *something for everyone.* Each one of us has the freedom to choose or reject this gift of salvation. We were born with the right to say no to the One who said yes to Calvary's Cross; but, in saying no, we also forfeit the right to be children of God. We may travel through life, but we can never be full of *life,* itself. For Jesus said, "I am the Way —yes, and the Truth and the *Life.* No one can get to the Father except by means of me." (*See* John 14:6, author's italics.)

A friend once gave me some poetic ideas which have served as an inspiration for my way to say it all.

Salvation

The Father thought it
Angels applaud it
Jesus brought it
His blood bought it
The Holy Spirit wrought it
The Bible taught it
The devil fought it
Sinners have sought it
Sinners have caught it
And hallelujah!
Happy is the child that can say
"I've got it!"

My friends, that kind of joyous assurance does not come from being pretty, or talented, or intelligent, or rich. It simply comes from being God's person.